Enabling Critical Pedagogy
in Higher Education

Mike Seal and Alan Smith

Series Editors: Joy Jarvis and Karen Smith

**CRITICAL PRACTICE IN
HIGHER EDUCATION**

First published in 2021 by Critical Publishing Ltd

British Library Cataloguing in Publication Data
A CIP record for this book is available from the British Library

ISBN: 978-1-914171-09-3

This book is also available in the following e-book formats:
EPUB ISBN: 978-1-914171-11-6
Adobe e-book ISBN: 978-1-914171-12-3

Cover design by Out of House Limited
Text design by Greensplash Limited
Project management by Newgen Publishing UK
Printed and bound in Great Britain by 4edge, Essex

Critical Publishing
3 Connaught Road
St Albans
AL3 5RX

www.criticalpublishing.com

Paper from responsible sources

Contents

Meet the authors and series editors

Mike Seal is Professor of Education and Social Mobility at the University of Suffolk and was previously a Reader in Critical Pedagogy at Newman University. His research areas are critical and queer pedagogy and social justice in higher education. He is a UK National Teaching Fellow, a Principal Fellow of the Higher Education Academy and a Fellow of the Royal Society of the Arts.

Alan Smith is responsible for both undergraduate and postgraduate courses in youth and community work and related areas at Leeds Beckett University. He is Vice-Chair of the National Youth Agency Education and Training Standards Committee (England) and co-chair of the Joint Education and Training Standards (JETS) committee for England, Scotland, Wales and all-Ireland. He is a UK National Teaching Fellow and a Senior Fellow of the Higher Education Academy.

Joy Jarvis is currently Professor of Educational Practice at the University of Hertfordshire and a UK National Teaching Fellow. She has experience in a wide range of educational contexts and works to create effective learning experiences for students and colleagues. She is particularly interested in the professional learning of those engaged in educational practice in higher education settings and has undertaken a range of projects, working with colleagues locally, nationally and internationally, to develop practice in teaching and leadership of teaching. Joy works with doctoral students exploring aspects of educational practice and encourages them to be adventurous in their methodological approaches and to share their findings in a range of contexts to enable practice change.

Karen Smith is Reader in Higher Education in the School of Education at the University of Hertfordshire. Her research focuses on how higher education policies and practices impact on those who work and study within universities. Karen has worked within educational development and on lecturer development programmes. She holds a Principal Fellowship of the Higher Education Academy and is currently the Director of the University of Hertfordshire's Professional Doctorate in Education. Karen also leads collaborative research and development in her School, where she engages in externally funded research and evaluation and supports the development of scholarly educational practice through practitioner research.

Book summary

This book argues that those working in higher education should embrace critical pedagogy as an essential critical approach that acts as a counter to individualising, consumerist and neoliberal visions of teaching and learning. Critical pedagogy aids lecturers and students in locating themselves within the evolving contemporary landscape of higher education. The book gives a comprehensive introduction to critical pedagogy, outlining its principles, aims and approaches, and offers a stepped approach to enabling it within higher education. It covers critical pedagogy's theoretical debates and critiques, and explores the tensions with trying to undertake it in higher education. Practical examples of enacting critical pedagogy are given in a variety of contexts: within the curriculum, within assessment, through learning and teaching, in the spaces in between and at an institutional level. The book offers hope that it is still possible to work with integrity as a critical pedagogue within the modern university.

Chapter 1 | An introduction to critical pedagogy

What is it?

Critical pedagogy has existed as an approach to education for almost 50 years, with antecedents going back much further than this, with roots in the enlightenment and working-class political education in the eighteenth century (Nicholls, 2017). It grew out of a concern among educationalists in the late 1960s with how education was being used as a method to reinscribe power relations in society, to create a 'common sense' that reinscribed dominant elites' social positions as 'natural and inevitable', and rather than to develop enquiring minds, to shut them down and make exclusive knowledge creation.

The aim of critical pedagogy is therefore to reverse this and illuminate the oppressed about their oppression. The ideas behind critical pedagogy, in its modern form, were described by Paulo Freire (1968) and since developed by authors such as Henry Giroux, Ira Shor, Michael Apple, Joe L Kincheloe, Shirley R Steinberg and Peter McLaren. It aims to give students, and people in general, the tools to undo, rethink and challenge their received wisdoms about what constitutes knowledge and education. Speaking to this book series, critical pedagogy has at its heart critical thinking.

Why is it important?

Thus described, critical pedagogy might sound like a concern for social scientists and perhaps the more radical end of education studies. However, critical pedagogy goes far deeper and wider than this. It goes right to the heart of the fundamental questions of what education is about, who is it for and how it is done, regardless of the subject being taught. It can also help the contemporary academic make sense of their place in the world.

Let us consider for a moment the predicament of the modern lecturer. Lecturing can be a lonely business. Many lecturers often feel ill-prepared for teaching and worry about this aspect of the job. Teaching is largely undertaken on our own, often without support or feedback, and in the UK we are measured on it via crude mechanisms such as the National Student Survey, module evaluations and the Teaching Excellence Framework. In this context, it is important because many of our students, and academics, feel increasingly disconnected from the passion that lead to them starting this journey. We can feel encouraged to teach to the lowest common denominator, to simplify everything, and to teach to the assessment criteria knowing we are judged by such crude measures as the National Student Survey and tick-box evaluations. We have heard many colleagues say they feel that we do not have time, and the students the inclination, to engage in wider, critical debate.

Academics also report feeling under siege in other ways, with an erosion of auto-nomy, democracy and accountability in their institutions. Neoliberalism and neo-managerialism have penetrated deep into academia, simultaneously constricting, intensifying and infantalising it. Examples include the expansion of workloads (Davies and Bansel, 2005; Hartman and Darab, 2012); a 'performativity' culture (Ball, 2012; Green, 2012); consumerist 'accountability' metrics (Bleiklie, 1998; Shore and Wright, 2004); heightened competition (Davies and Bansel, 2007; Nixon, 2011), and the commodification and instrumentalisation of knowledge and educational goals (Ball, 2012; Bullen et al, 2010; Nixon, 2011).

Many academics similarly report a dumbing down of their research, through how they apply for funding, what they can get funding for, and where and how they are expected to disseminate it. Critical pedagogy hopefully offers a way that we can connect and reconnect with our subject and our teaching, and make for a better experience for our students and ourselves. This book assesses whether critical pedagogy as an approach has potential resonance with educationalists looking for 'another way', who wish to make education vital and relevant again. Critical pedagogy can also offer academics a way of reconnecting with ourselves, of understanding our own positions in society and within our institutions, contextualising and mediating the forces modern academics are subject to. We, in turn, can be a part of the process of enabling students to consider their own positionalities. Most importantly, critical pedagogy offers hope. Hope to sustain us in difficult times when the aforementioned forces seem to become overwhelming, and we cannot see a way through them.

Why now?

We live in interesting times in higher education. The Covid crisis has entailed a rethink of what constitutes the classroom, and in turn questions the relative roles students, tutors, and power relations the pedagogic process. KPMG, one of the most neoliberal in the new private sector players in the higher education sector, opened their 2020 report 'The future of higher education in a disruptive world' with the following:

The Golden Age of universities in the developed world is passing and life is becoming tougher. Rising costs are no longer matched by a willingness of governments and students to pay for them. And yet the traditional operating model of a university cannot produce sufficient productivity gains to cover the gap.

(KPMG, 2020, p 2)

The report calls for wholesale change in pedagogy, curriculum and assessment, and a new relationship with students and the outside world. A half-hearted move to blended learning will not do; a transformation is needed. Neoliberals will undoubtedly, as the report starts to do, develop an individualised consumerist interpretation of what this transformation could mean. Those of us that want an alternative need to be able to articulate what this could look like and build for it. We do not want a return to the status quo because the status quo perpetuated certain privileges and institutionalised structural discrimination against disadvantaged groups (Seal, 2021).

The structure of the book

The aims of this book are to:

» provide a comprehensive introduction to enabling critical pedagogy in higher education;

» explore the theoretical debates and tensions entailed in such an endeavour;

» give practical examples of enabling critical pedagogy at an institutional level, within the curriculum, within assessment, through learning and teaching and in the spaces in between;

» outline the conditions for critical pedagogy to be able to flourish within higher education.

The book intends to facilitate the active engagement of the reader. As such we highlight examples, critical issues, critical questions for practice and end of chapter summaries. The book comprises seven chapters. The rest of this first chapter explores some of the key themes of critical pedagogy, including its principles, aims, approaches and steps to enact it. Chapter 2 explores the possibilities of enacting critical pedagogy in curriculum design. Chapter 3 discusses enacting critical pedagogy in assessment. Chapter 4 discusses enacting critical pedagogy in learning and teaching. Chapter 5 explores other spaces and initiatives within the university where critical pedagogy can happen and be encouraged. Chapter 6 explores the possibilities and conditions for being a critical pedagogue within higher education, giving a useful set of criteria for an institution to consider in supporting critical pedagogy. The final chapter serves as a conclusion. It argues that it is possible to enact critical pedagogy within higher education, even at a structural level, although we need to be realistic about the limitations. It returns to the principles, aims and approaches of critical pedagogy and reflects on the steps to be taken.

Principles, aims and approaches of critical pedagogy

Critical pedagogy has a set of underlying principles, a set of aims and suggested approaches. As Figure 1.1 indicates, these all stem from, and nestle within, each other. Throughout the book we will relate the examples given back to these principles, aims and approaches.

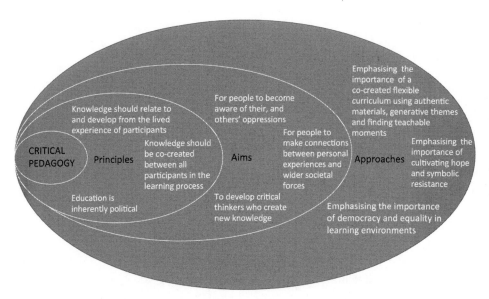

Figure 1.1 Principles, aims and approaches of critical pedagogy.

Principles

Education is inherently political

Critical pedagogy seeks to de-neutralise education and knowledge creation and acknowledge it is inherently political, particularly where it concerns human relations. A common association with knowledge, and particularly theory, is that it is something created or discovered by 'objective', 'neutral' 'experts', often under sci-entific conditions. This scientific approach, useful for understanding the material world, is conflated to humans. Education is traditionally seen as a 'banking', 'neutral' process whereby this 'objective' knowledge is transferred, via a teacher who knows it, to students who do not. The process of students absorbing this knowledge is called learning. Students are not encouraged to question the knowledge they receive. Crucially, when a student applies this learning to their experiences and finds that it does not tally, they have either not understood the knowledge correctly, or not applied it correctly, or their experiences are not representative, and nobody is ever encouraged to question the validity or truth of what has been taught.

Knowledge should relate to and develop from the lived experience of participants

Traditionally, knowledge and theory making is abstracted from most people's everyday lived experience. For critical pedagogues, theory needs to relate to the lived experiences of people, and where it does not, we need to change it for the better. One word for this is praxis, and critical pedagogy has consistently described itself as a praxis (Batsleer, 2012; Ord, 2000; Smith, 1994). Praxis is often interpreted as the synthesis of theory and action. However, it is more complex, subtle and radical than this. Critical pedagogy has a dynamic, dialectical view of how knowledge is created (Aristotle, 1976). It sees knowledge as an evolving thing (Carr and Kemmis, 1989), and this needs to be shared with students.

Example 1.1

Sharing the nature of knowledge with students

Relevant principles: *knowledge should be co-created between all participants in the learning process.*

Relevant aims: *to develop critical thinkers who create new knowledge.*

Relevant approaches: *emphasising the importance of democracy and equality in learning environments.*

As educators we sometimes hear students groan when we don't give them the answers: why are we making it hard for them, can we not just tell them what is right? A critical pedagogue's response would be that this is not us being awkward. Behind this refusal is a powerful thought about education – that knowledge is not static; it is dynamic. It is created through dialogue. In a very real sense we cannot tell students what is right, for there is rarely a right. Sometimes the student will know more than we do, and we should acknowledge this and let them educate us. We have to create and contest knowledge together.

Knowledge should be co-created between all participants in the learning process

Critical pedagogues view knowledge as something we create through dialogue with each other. Cho (2010) describes knowledge as *'democratic, context-dependent, and appreciative of the value of learners' cultural heritage'* (p 315). The creation of this evolving knowledge is an active democratic process that entails interrogation of the world by all parties. This means not simply acknowledging the diversity and multiculturalism in the room, as this would construct people's views of cultures, including their own, as monolithic. Critical pedagogy may well entail challenging and changing cultural norms (Freire, 1970a, p 12). Being oppressed does not make one less subject to dominant hegemonies.

Aims of critical pedagogy

To develop critical thinkers who create new knowledge

The most important thing we are doing as educators is enabling people to become critical thinkers – knowledge creators, able to apply and synthesise new ideas and information into new ways of thinking as situations change and evolve. The break between experience, practice and theory needs to be challenged and students need to see how they have a right and duty to create new knowledge. However, this is not an easy process. For learning to be critical is, and should be, challenging, particularly as the first thing we need to do is challenge our own assumptions about learning and re-evaluate our previous experiences of it. People are distanced from their natural critical thinking skills and at the same time encouraged to think individualistically about their views, as though they are commodities to which they have a right. Both sides of this need to be challenged. As illustrated below, consumerisation can extend, and manifest, in interactions in the classroom.

Example 1.2

Challenging the consumer dynamic

Relevant principles: *education is inherently political. Knowledge should relate to and develop from the lived experience of participants.*

Relevant aims: *to develop critical thinkers who create new knowledge. For people to make connections between personal experiences and wider societal forces.*

Relevant approaches: *emphasising the importance of democracy and equality in learning environments. Cultivating hope and symbolic resistance.*

This challenge has been ever more apparent in the UK, with the impact of student loans and the emphasis on consumer practices embodied by the Competition and Marketing Authority's interest in higher education. This commodification has led to a growing individualisation, which in turn creates a sense that everyone can assert their individual right to voice an opinion and then closing down any opportunity to engender a learning opportunity when students say, after asserting something, *'well that's what I think'*, quickly followed by *'I am entitled to my opinion.'* A critical pedagogue's response could go along the lines of *'sorry, but in our spaces, this isn't good enough – you have to defend your opinions, be open to change, and sometimes have the bravery to stand alone.'*

For people to become aware of their, and others', oppressions

For Freire, becoming a critical thinker entails 'conscientisation'. Drawing on Gramsci, critical pedagogues work to encourage students to *'develop a critical consciousness of who they are and what their language represents by examining questions of language, culture, and history through the lens of power'* (Brito et al, 2004, p 23). They need to become aware of their own oppression, and by extension understand how others are oppressed. However, this is no simple process.

Critical issues

Who determines when and how someone is oppressed?

There are issues with the idea of conscientisation, particularly the idea of 'false consciousness', a term developed by Engels, not Marx, whereby people are not aware of their own oppression. Rancière (1992) critiqued Bourdieu for privileging the role of the intellectual and condemning the masses as unknowing and in need of liberation. Instead, Rancière views the working class as inherently capable of learning and developing intellect. However, they have been led to believe that they are not intelligent by a hegemonic system that deliberately undermines their self-belief. In addition, they may have lost the will to use their analytic abilities, in the face of seemingly monolithic social forces where they have been forced to prioritise short-term survival.

$\longrightarrow$

For Rancière the pedagogue should act under the assumption that we are all intelligent enough to understand the world, and that, given access to resources, we can discern the knowledge that will facilitate this understanding. He invites the pedagogue to become ignorant, not that they deny their knowledge, or hide it, but they should not privilege it – we should uncouple our mastery from our knowledge. The role of the educator is two-fold. First, to act on the students' will, self-belief and efficacy, the will to engage and challenge themselves and others, and to wish to learn. Second, an educator's role is to attend to the content of what argument people are creating, but only in terms of ensuring people's arguments have logic and internal consistency, but that they attend to, understand and deconstruct the language behind those arguments and the concepts behind the language. This entails gaining access to resources, often intellectual resources, but it does not mean we determine the content of those resources.

For people to make connections between personal experiences and wider societal forces

Freire (1970b) names three levels of consciousness: intransitive, semi-transitive and critical consciousness. Those with an intransitive consciousness accept their lives as they are and take the view that any changes are for reasons beyond their control and seen as fate. Those with a semi-transitive consciousness are aware of their problems and still think of them as inevitable, but they may think they can change things on a local level. Actions are therefore often localised and short term. It is only when people have a critical consciousness that they see the structural dimensions of their problems, making connections between their problems and the social context in which these problems are embedded, both in terms of analysis and actions that will challenge their structural oppressions as well as addressing some of their immediate concerns.

Approaches in critical pedagogy

Emphasising the importance of democracy and equality in learning environments

For critical pedagogues, learners have their own theories and ideas about the world, and this needs to be our starting place (Bolton, 2010). Similarly, critical pedagogues need to challenge the colonisation of democracy in education through its construction as consumerism. Under this construction, education needs to be delivered in a way that students like, and say things that they like, supposedly measured through things like the UK's National Student Survey – this is again not critical pedagogy, or a true informed democracy, which would both be very challenging. Critical pedagogues need to deconstruct with the student how consumerism is a constricting and deceptive form of democracy that placates rather than liberates.

Being truly democratic can be difficult for some educators as it means they have to acknowledge and challenge the structures they operate within, including the power and privilege it bestows on them – the '*power which is given to them through their titles*' (Foley, 2007). We need to be explicitly humble and challenging of our own privilege, any deference we get. We also need to disrupt learners' passivity in their relationships with us and each other. As Joldersma (1999) notes, there is a certain familiar complacency in this for learners; they can sit back and receive, not taking responsibility for their learning, or the learning environment. Some learners passively resist, as they may have done at school, taking small chances to undermine the authority of the teacher. However, this can be in a non-constructive way that can in turn be infantalised by the teacher. We can also go too far too soon, as the example below illustrates.

Example 1.3

The need to take time; liberation is rarely instant

Relevant principles: *education is inherently political. Knowledge should be co-created between all participants in the learning process.*

Relevant aims: *to develop critical thinkers who create new knowledge. For people to become aware of their, and others', oppressions and develop the will to act.*

Relevant approaches: *emphasising a co-created flexible curriculum using authentic materials, generative themes and finding teachable moments. Cultivating hope and symbolic resistance.*

Mike remembers once teaching a group of master's students a module focusing on critical pedagogy and during the introductory session was going through the learning outcomes as is common practice. He was suddenly struck by the irony of reading these out when critical pedagogy was the antithesis of this. He ripped up the piece of paper he was reading and said that the group should come up with their own curriculum and learning outcomes and he would then take it to a module approval panel. He left them alone for an hour to do this, but when he came back they had got the paper he had ripped up out of the bin and were trying to put it back together – he had pushed them too quickly and too far out of their comfort zone.

Emphasising a co-created flexible curriculum using authentic materials, generative themes and finding teachable moments

Some of the fundamental techniques within critical pedagogy that flow from these principles are having a flexible curriculum with authentic materials, finding teachable moments and discovering generative themes.

Flexible curriculum and using authentic materials

A fundamental within critical and emancipatory education is that no one methodology can work for all cultures, populations and situations (Degener, 2001). All decisions related to curricula, including the material to be studied, should be based on the needs, interests, experiences and situations of students (Giroux, 2012; Shor, 1992). Furthermore, students, as Giroux (2012) puts it, should be active participants in designing and correcting the curricula – most fundamentally the curriculum needs to relate to the lived social and economic lives of the learner, and help them move from the micro of their situations and crises to see the wider social-economic forces behind them, and their contradictions (Degener, 2001).

Furthermore, the materials used for education should come from and have resonance with people's everyday lives and include books poems, films and adverts (Keesing-Styles, 2003; Kincheloe, 2005; Ohara et al, 2000). They can be equally brought to the table by tutors and students, and especially students as their consciousness develops. It is in linking people's everyday experiences and crises to wider socio-economic forces that people start to see *'both the reproductive nature and the possibility of resistance to problematic content'* (Aliakbari and Faraji, 2011, p 80).

Generative themes

Taking this further is the idea of generative themes (Aliakbari and Faraji, 2011). This is where the group, in deciding the curriculum and theme to be explored, is seeking themes with certain characteristics. Themes should firstly be a galvanising force for the community, something about which there is passion and feelings. Secondly, the theme must have tensions and contradictions within it, things that do not add up that need to be worked through and have a potential to create something new that resolves these tensions. These tensions should not be allowed to become negative, but their energy turned into a positive incentive to change. Generative themes should also open up discussion about, and relate to, wider social issues. In doing so they can lead to the opening up of other generative themes (ie a generative theme has the seed of other generative themes within it). Finally, generative themes must have the potential for action, that something concrete can be done about them. An illustration of how this has been done is outlined below.

Example 1.4

From individual experience to collective action

Relevant principles: *education is inherently political. Knowledge should relate to and develop from the lived experience of participants.*

Relevant aims: *to develop critical thinkers who create new knowledge. For people to make connections between personal experiences and wider societal forces.*

Relevant approaches: *emphasising a co-created flexible curriculum using authentic materials, generative themes and finding teachable moments.*

Within the foundation year, Mike would get students to explore their own educational experiences, and to not see themselves as in deficit. They then explore higher education and look at who it is for and how it is structured. A field trip is organised to Oxford, both the university and the city, and many students experience a visceral sense of contradictions and unease, aware of their own lack of social capital, coterminous with a belief that they have a right to higher education. This is then unpacked back at the university and has meant that a number of students have become engaged in challenging the Augar report (2019), which is a direct threat to foundation years and widening participation. The post-18 review was announced in February 2018. Since then the independent panel, chaired by Philip Augar, undertook an extensive programme of stakeholder engagement and evidence gathering. This report sets out their findings and policy recommendations for government consideration.

Teachable moments

One of the characteristics of critical pedagogy is the ability to think in the moment and improvise (Seal and Harris, 2014; Smith, 1994). This can mean recognising that a particular session plan is not working, or having resonance, and adjusting it accordingly. On another level this can mean spotting and seizing an opportunity to relate a discussion to wider issues. However, the responsibility for this should not lie with the pedagogue alone. Key features of Mike's foundation year include three hours of curriculum-free student-led small group tutorials a week. This is cited by students as one of the transformative elements of the course.

Emphasising the importance of cultivating hope and symbolic resistance

One of the dangers of critical pedagogy is that while it is good at critique, it leaves us with little hope. Freire always came back to hope, seeing it as a fundamental part of being human: *'Hope is an ontological need ... I am hopeful, not out of mere stubbornness, but out of an existential concrete imperative'* (2004, p 2). For Freire hope is part of the human condition; the role of education is not conceived as one of instilling hope but rather of evoking it (Webb, 2010). Freire warns that the hope of the progressive educator cannot be that of *'an irresponsible adventurer'* (2004, p 77). Several times in his writings Freire equates hope with waiting – not the passive waiting of one who folds their arms in resignation, but the 'active waiting' of one who persistently seeks and struggles (Freire, 2004). Mike has commented on this elsewhere as one of the reasons we should try to enable critical pedagogy within higher education.

We should not fall into traps of thinking that if the rebellion does not take power, the revolution does not succeed, we have failed. Foucault taught us that power plays out at lots of levels, so by definition it can be contested at those levels – and will eventually start to falter at them.

(Seal, 2014, p 134)

Conclusion: how critical pedagogy can be enabled – a step process

Critical pedagogy could seem an intimidating project, or one simply out of reach of the average lecturer, who often does not have, or at least feel they have, much institutional influence, let alone potential wider impact. We see enabling critical pedagogy in higher education as a step process. It is fine to stay at the first step. You will become part of a process of change. We also hope that this slightly frustrates you and you start thinking about engaging with steps two and three. There is step four, where critical pedagogues start coming together and supporting each other in changing our whole institutions and the sector radically. We have not outlined this step because it has yet to happen, and how to do this needs to be worked out collectively.

Step one: change how you teach and your relationship with students

Change what you can within the restrictions you have. Often, as a lecturer, we are given a module, with set learning outcomes, a set curriculum and a set assessment. We have even heard of colleagues who have their PowerPoints and learning materials scrutinised, with quality assurance and even consumer management assurance given as reasons (neither of these regimes ask for these things in fact). However, they cannot control what happens in the classroom, how we manage the PowerPoints we may have been given, and how we spin off them and work with student comments and contributions. If you do this, students will respond and 'engage' and 'participate' more, all things that higher education struggles with. They will also often do better in terms of marks and retention as a result, again things that will give you leverage.

Step two: push the structure as far as you can and build alliances

Once you have some success, you will have the leverage to build on what you are doing, mainly because you are dovetailing with institutional priorities. All assessment criteria and learning objectives are interpretable and we have given examples of how people have worked within these constrictions. Learning objectives are full of vagaries such as 'exploring relevant social policy and theories', or 'describe the Universe and explain and interpret the evidence base for the description' (taken from an astrophysics module). Who determines what is relevant, or counts as evidence, does not have to come from the lecturer.

As lecturers we need to move away from thinking 'how do I get across to students the information I know they need to know?' to thinking 'how do we explore what information is relevant, and how can we find out about it, together?' Assessments are often reviewed annually, and courses revalidated every five years. This means you will have opportunities to change the structures you work within. It is possible to say that the learning objectives and assessment will be negotiated with students; you just have to win over quality assurance professionals as to why this is needed and see them as an ally. All this will mean winning over colleagues, who will be naturally curious about what you are doing, particularly if it is seen to be working.

Step three: be seen as a pedagogic expert, internally and externally

While being an expert is in some ways an anathema to the critical pedagogue, you may need to become an expert in deconstructing the idea of being an expert. This means engaging with the teaching and learning process of the university, getting recognition for teaching through schemes such as the Advance HE Fellowships and awards such as National Teaching Fellowships in the UK for your expertise in critical pedagogy. It also means writing, and there are plenty of publishers and journals that will be interested in your work. It also means taking research opportunities – most universities have funds for undertaking staff–student partnerships, and these are perfect for enacting critical pedagogy.

Reach out to colleagues; all universities will have centres for learning and teaching, who will help you set up groups and events. Present at the learning and teaching conference all institutions have – offer to run a strand, even the whole thing. Similarly, you can present what you have been doing externally – there is the British and American Educational Research Associations (BERA and AERA), the Society for Research into Higher Education and many subject-based associations, which often also run special interest groups. At this point you may also want to consider career progression, either as a programme leader, giving you much more scope to develop courses with critical pedagogy embedded, or going down the professorial route, meaning you will have much scope in influencing – there are now routes to becoming a professor in learning and teaching, but this still entails undertaking pedagogic research and publications, which you have started to do.

Critical questions for practice

» How could you expose and deconstruct your power in the classroom? How would you feel about doing this?

» How can you meaningfully involve your students in creating their own curriculum?

» Can you think of a generative theme that has arisen in your classroom recently, something that has the seeds to open up wider questions and make wider links?

» Can you think about a teachable moment you have had, when you have decided to act on a student comment in the moment and take the lecture in a different direction?

Summary

- The focus of critical pedagogy is to co-create critical reflectors who can recognise their own oppression, deconstruct prevailing hegemonies in education and expose its political nature.

- It believes knowledge should be rooted in the experience of everyone and knowledge creation is an organic democratic process that necessitates the breaking down of barriers between teachers, learners and knowledge creators and cultivating hope.

- Its techniques include having a curriculum negotiated with learners and using authentic materials from their experience, developing generative themes that open up discussion about, and relate to, wider social issues, building on spontaneous teachable moments.

Useful texts

Freire, P (1972) *Pedagogy of the Oppressed.* Harmondsworth: Penguin.

The classic critical pedagogy text giving an exploration of dialogue and the possibilities for liberatory practice. Freire seeks to transform the relationship between students, teachers and society. Freire introduces the highly influential notion of banking education, highlights the contrasts between education forms that treat people as objects rather than subjects and explores education as action.

Freire, P (1995) *Pedagogy of Hope: Reliving Pedagogy of the Oppressed* . New York: Continuum.

This book began as a new preface to his classic work. Its importance lies in Freire's reflection on the text and how it was received, and on the development of policy and practice subsequently and the importance of cultivating hope for critical pedagogues. He argues that although hope alone is not enough to achieve liberation, without hope there is no struggle at all.

Giroux, H A (2020) *On Critical Pedagogy.* London: Bloomsbury Publishing.

In this book, Giroux analyses the increasingly empirical orientation of teaching, focusing on the culture of positivism, and examines some of the major economic, social and political forces undermining the promise of democratic schooling in both public and higher education. He argues against the tendency by both right wing and neoliberal interests to reduce schooling to training, and students merely to customers. Giroux also considers the legacy of Freire and issues a fundamental challenge to educators, public intellectuals and others who believe in the promise of radical democracy.

Introduction

By now, we are sure you can see opportunities and challenges for enacting critical pedagogy in the curriculum, and in particular the balancing act of academic quality assurance, benchmarking and more general issues of validation requirements. In this chapter, examples will be given of innovative ways in which students have been involved in validations, and in designing 'credit-bearing modules', where students have the opportunity to create their own curriculum. It will also explore how deconstructing people's experiences of the education system, and their conception of knowledge creation, can be built into the curriculum itself.

Applying critical pedagogy to the curriculum

In seeking to move towards a more embedded approach, it is important to differentiate the varying levels at which we can adopt critical pedagogy in terms of curriculum, and its planning, with a particular focus on the role students can play. Catherine Bovill, writing specifically about student co-creation in higher education, tackles this issue in a number of articles (2014 onwards) and in her recent book in this series (Bovill, 2020). In Bovill's work with Cherie Woolmer (2019), she addresses the issue of co-creation of the curriculum as different to co-creation in the curriculum; and while she may not explicitly be writing about critical pedagogy, the underpinning values and assumptions are firmly rooted in this tradition.

Bovill and Woolmer (2019) press this further by saying that it is important we develop a *'deeper understanding of how curriculum is conceptualised in higher education [as this] can help us to be more explicit about what we are inviting students to co-create and ultimately, may influence the types of co-creation that are possible'* (p 409). They go on to add a further footnote,

[the ...] term co-created curriculum is commonly misused to describe co-creation of co-curricular or extracurricular activity. In some cases, this may be explained by some confusion over the terms co-created curriculum and co-curriculum, but in many other instances, there is a curious oxymoron where people are using the term co-created curriculum to refer to collaborative extracurricular initiatives outside academic curricula.

(ibid, p 409)

For us, it is the opportunity that critical pedagogy offers to reshape and reform the curriculum in its entirety, both what we teach and how we teach it, that offers the greatest potential to bring about this much-needed change.

Within this chapter, we will seek to show how small step changes to the way we conceptualise the curriculum and its teaching can move from enacting critical pedagogy in the curriculum and see it move to critical pedagogy as and of the curriculum. We will offer you examples of how all participants can shape a lesson or module, taking control of the content and delivery, through to seeing students and others as equal partners in the design, validation and approval of whole awards. But if it is so easy, and you believe it is meaningful and worthwhile, why hasn't it happened before?

Critical issues

Is higher education ready for critical pedagogy?

I'm sure, like us, you have heard a lot of self-censoring from colleagues on building critical pedagogy into the curriculum in higher education. A common refrain is that 'quality' structures do not allow for such innovation, with their demand for aims, learning outcomes, predetermined teaching strategies and set assessments, etc. However, in many cases colleagues have not actually tried; they have all too often self-censored that they would not be allowed to embed critical pedagogy, or other innovations. When Alan facilitated a recent staff development workshop, the vast majority of participants described module descriptors as too inflexible, yet when they are reviewed they are less a straitjacket and more a framework, often without the very rigid constraints we all imagine.

At Leeds Beckett University, the Centre for Learning and Teaching is leading a university-wide review of inclusivity in course design, development and assessment; it asks questions of course teams about the breadth of resources used (seeking to address the issue of a colonised, predominately white and male authorship), the 'voice' of students in design, delivery and enhancement, and finally the accessibility and inclusivity of assessment choices. None of this is acknowledged as critical pedagogy, but certainly its underpinning principles, aims and general approaches are moving in that direction.

For many, the obvious challenge when faced with questioning the existing models of curriculum design and delivery come from our shared experience of education to date. Whether that is school, the place where the curriculum has been constructed to maintain a status quo, to replicate established norms and to ultimately 'teach' young people (in particular) how to fit in to society, rather than question it or challenge any of the power-holders' assumptions; or further and higher education where many students are encouraged to focus their learning on a future career, being 'taught' what is already known and done. As Freire (1968) would describe, a banking model of education that seeks to domesticate. This power imbalance is replicated throughout most neoliberal models of education, and as our introduction suggests, this is at the heart of the contradictions and challenges when considering how to enact critical pedagogy within the academe.

The controlling hand of curriculum

In order to start to address these concerns, it is perhaps best if we think about how curriculum is defined and constructed. For many, we base our understanding on our common experiences of schooling, a model of curriculum which is about control. Control of the syllabus, both its content and delivery, but more than that, control of the 'product' and implicitly assessment, as it claims the power to decide who has met the 'product' standards contained within the curriculum. These two versions of curriculum will be common to many.

1 Curriculum as syllabus, embedded within a more traditional form of education, which dictates and defines the transmission of very specific content.

2 Curriculum as product, the basis of education in all sectors and professions, and at most levels, when we consider the language of competencies and learning outcomes; even the developmental milestones of early childhood development.

But as critical educators, whose practices are shaped and informed by a more radical stance, as described by Freire, we want to see education that liberates, that empowers and is informed by the experiences of active and willing participants.

Example 2.1

Starting to think about 'power' in the learning environment

Relevant principles: *knowledge should be co-created between all participants in the learning process.*

Relevant aims: *for people to make connections between personal experiences and wider societal forces.*

Relevant approaches: *the importance of democracy and equality in learning environments.*

When Alan introduces Freirean approaches to students, he asks them to do quite a simple reflective task, as it offers a starting point to their thinking about learning, and questions the power structures that exist within higher education, and the classroom more generally.

1   Think of three things you can say you have learned since leaving formal education (this might be driving a car, bringing up a family, managing your finances).

2   Choose one of these, and ask yourself the following questions.

   »   Why did you 'learn' it?

   »   Who helped you 'learn' it?

   »   What was your relationship to the person who helped?

   »   What was the basis of that relationship – financial, work-related, etc?

For the majority of adults who reflect on their post-compulsory education and learning, we use a very different set of reference points to formal education: we often talk about relational pedagogy, or a process of learning, the implicit benefit and pleasure of learning – and ultimately, we attach meaning and value because we have ownership of the process.

Building on this reflection, Freire's empowering model of education and curriculum doesn't seek to impose a set of already dominant values, and replicate what is known, but it challenges learners to find their own solutions, fostering creativity and action, using problem-based learning to generate learning. This model of curriculum has a different starting point, and a very different value base.

» Curriculum as process, where the curriculum is emergent, there are no definite or predetermined outcomes, but maybe a framework in which they should loosely fit, a curriculum where understanding develops through the process of doing and learning.

» Curriculum as praxis, building on the process model, seeks to question and challenge everyone involved to question the assumptions and beliefs that might underpin the learning, and ultimately it questions the curriculum itself (adapted from Ord, 2008).

These latter two versions of curriculum are especially problematic for a system of education based on a hierarchy of knowledge, and a bureaucracy of process that seeks to protect and maintain higher education in high regard, unquestioned, unchallenged and ultimately built not only to protect the status quo, but also to privilege those groups already in positions of power and authority. It is through recognising these tensions that anyone who wishes to practise any form of critical pedagogy must find a personal and professional position that is comfortable for them and has integrity. Especially when the critical pedagogue already has their 'status' and must ensure that their learners have a curriculum on offer that meets any external benchmarks, and conforms to their institution's own quality assurance regime, and the needs of the 'consumer' – students who may not even be aware of the liberating potential of critical pedagogy.

For both of us, it is our experience of working in youth and community work during the late 1980s and early 1990s, when we saw the challenges faced when curriculum is imposed, without recognising that the values and ethics which underpin our profession are built on models of empowerment and overcoming oppression. At that time, the UK Conservative Government had already overseen the implementation of a national curriculum within schools, and was attempting to define, and in doing so, limit, the curriculum offered by youth workers in their everyday practices. The neoliberal, New World Order was dictating that education, like every other commodity, must be judged in terms of its *Value For Money* and measured against a set of externally driven targets or measures. As Giroux and Giroux (2006) describe '... *a tension between democratic values and market values, between dialogic engagement and rigid authoritarianism*' (p 21). In an attempt to respond to these tensions, youth and community work embraced the notion of curriculum as a process rather than just product, something which Eileen Newman and Gina Ingram recognised in 1989, and which Jon Ord extended further in 2008. In both cases, they recognised the need to use the language of curriculum, but to define it in a way that was neither straitjacket nor outcome driven. In doing so, they created a debate and a multiplicity of definitions that ultimately allows us to imbue the values and practices of critical pedagogy within higher education.

Although it is at the point when we try to enact critical pedagogy in our daily practices that the 'straitjackets' and self-censorship start to emerge, and doubt creeps in. Yet we have good working relationships with colleagues in our institutional quality teams, and recognise and value the significance of external validity and transparency. Mike often describes that as long as you take the approach that you have something you would like to do or a challenge to overcome, you can work with institutional policy and procedures and forward-thinking colleagues in quality assurance and quality enhancement to bring their expertise to help you make it work.

Example 2.2

Critical pedagogy within a module

Relevant principles: *knowledge should relate to and develop from the lived experience of participants.*

Relevant aims: *to develop critical thinkers who create new knowledge.*

Relevant approaches: *the importance of democracy and equality in learning environments.*

Mike describes the creation of a second-year module called Contemporary Issues in Youth and Community Work (which is the degree students are undertaking). In the module, students identify an area of the overall subject that they would like to explore; they have to come up with the learning outcomes and outline the curriculum they would like to be taught. They finally design the assessment that will 'test' their learning. In terms of dovetailing with the overall learning outcomes of the programme, this approach sees students testing many of their transferable skills: to problem solve, design programmes, critically analyse and ultimately to be able to understand the theoretical terrain of their subject. Thirty per cent of the available marks are reserved for the testing of these abilities to come up with learning outcomes, a coherent curriculum and a meaningful assessment task. In their second year students do similarly in a module on critical pedagogy – the difference being that the terrain of the module has to be broadly within that of the curriculum of critical pedagogy – something which requires them to both understand its underpinning principles, its challenges and ultimately the freedom which it can create.

$\longrightarrow$

The experiences of students undertaking the above module have been written up by two colleagues of Mike's (the publication is recommended at the end of this chapter), but one of the most interesting debates that emerged with the students was about this sense of freedom. Students reported really struggling with the freedom they had, and with being able to determine the content of the module, and the shift in power and responsibility in the learning relationship. As one student said:

I don't know if it was that I was scared of freedom, or it was that we didn't know what to do, I think that was the main thing, we didn't know where to start. I think it was a mixture of both to be honest wasn't it. People, I think, me personally, I think I was scared of freedom 'cause I like control, I like to know where the boundaries are.

This example shows how we can encourage students to feel empowered, helping guide and shape their own education and learning, but as Bovill and Woolmer (2019) describe, this is, at best, co-creation in the curriculum (p 409). It may be enough to encourage students to feel more empowered, and with that feeling of success comes a confidence to engage in further acts of critical pedagogy, but is that enough? Does it give voice to the individual participants; can it remove the hidden reality of power: the dominant ideologies contained within our key texts, the power to assess and ultimately pass or fail a student, and our institutional policies and procedures which bring scrutiny to bear on all our practices?

It is against this backdrop, those first tentative steps of enacting critical pedagogy in the curriculum, that we must also reflect on the power we have as educators, part of the system which our practices may be seeking to challenge. In Chapter 1, Mike has already talked about his early experiences of enacting critical pedagogy with master's students (Example 1.3). It was a module he had inherited and, like many critical pedagogy modules, critical pedagogy was the territory, but did not inform the module beyond this. When Mike returned to find his group trying to piece together the learning objectives he had ripped up. He had pushed people too quickly, too soon. Apparently, freedom is something that needs to be brought in gradually, and even with that caveat, there is a debate about what degree of freedom people have in determining the curriculum of a module, or more explicitly the curriculum of their entire learning. As students explain, while they may welcome the freedom to determine the curriculum and assessment, they still need to have an assessment and a 'mark'!

Did we have freedom? Did we really? Or did you give us freedom to a certain extent and make us believe that we had freedom but in actual fact it wasn't freedom because then we had to produce an assignment which had to be produced in some sort of certain ways to give us a mark.

(module feedback)

In fact, in Example 1.3, one group rebelled against the freedom offered and rejected assessment altogether – though ultimately backtracking as they wanted their degrees. Perhaps this is more about how the module was set up, and too much freedom was promised. Bardy and Gilsenen (2021) worry about how genuine and authentic their experiment was, to enact critical pedagogy in the curriculum, when it doesn't exist beyond the freedom of a single module, is to raise a false hope and create an inherent tension. In managing the Contemporary Issues in Youth and Community Work module, we think their experiment was legitimate and evoked a debate in critical pedagogy around idealism and realism, but did it enact critical pedagogy or change practice, however minimally?

It is fair to say that Freire (1974) never thought that we are free, or should seek freedom, seeing it as escapist and utopian. We cannot exist in contexts devoid of power and restrictions. Conversely, he challenges us to acknowledge our restrictions and recognise power dynamics, and yet to find hope and authenticity and political autonomy within whatever situation we are in, not matter how oppressive. He would not say we should always be practical and accepting – indeed we should continually push and expand the boundaries, and having ideals can help and nourish us in this – but we are not free, otherwise we would not be oppressed.

This equally applies to us – we should not project our hopelessness onto the quality mechanisms of universities; we can use them creatively and get authenticity out of them. Neither should we give up totally on higher education and say that enclaves such as the new co-operative university initiatives are the only authentic route. They are great, and can act as sources of inspiration and hope, but we need to take that hope back into the mainstream, to hold a mirror to universities to truly be the places their strategic plans espouse.

Perhaps to be authentic, if we are to promise more autonomy to students, and to genuinely embrace the values and practices of education which empowers, we must help everyone gain both confidence and understanding in how they approach critical pedagogy in the curriculum. Much like riding a bike, we first need to gain self-confidence before the stabilisers are removed, or that supportive hand is taken from the shoulder. Maybe to enact critical pedagogy as curriculum is to 'teach' it, recognising that courses have levels, not only to impose structure or maintain rigour and integrity, but also to reflect a view that learning is developmental, and like climbing a tall building, it needs scaffolding.

Taking this idea of scaffolding a stage further, it is perhaps important that we recognise and remember our students have come from an education system that embraced a particular model of scaffolding, one that is all about control. Not merely the content and delivery of the curriculum, but the choice of subjects to be studied, the sources that are valued and credible, to recognise the inherent class-based values they seek to impose (Bernstein) and the hidden hand of neo-liberalism, where employability and value for money have become the measures of success. Think back to the earlier reflective task and consider how you would answer if the reflection was about a school-based subject such as mathematics or physics.

Perhaps the best way to expose this scaffolding, and challenge the stranglehold of bureaucracy, is to consider our existing model of curriculum and how we engage with course development and validation or revalidation.

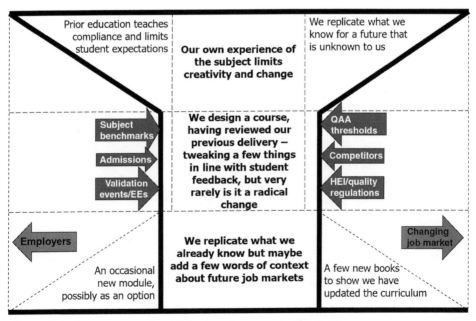

Figure 2.1 A representation of the 'curriculum straitjacket'.

In the model of curriculum shown in Figure 2.1, you may feel that it embraces and addresses a great many factors, but we would argue that these are instantly limited by both our students' experience of education – based on a 'banking' model, alongside our own sense of knowing – again this is limited by what 'we' already have knowledge and experience of. In developing the model above, we wanted to show not only the 'hard lines' of explicit 'control' that are exerted, but also the dotted lines, which are implicit and shape or limit our willingness to be radical or creative; these are often the unquestioned assumptions and beliefs about what is possible, and the power we assign to the other factors which are at play:

» Subject Benchmarks, defining what makes up the integrity of a named award or subject discipline;

» Quality Assurance Agency threshold criteria, predetermined 'scaffolding' that defines both level and expectation;

» sector norms, what are our 'competitors' doing; we feel the need to comply with sector expectations rather than take risks – the cold hand of marketisation;

» admission, institutional criteria about which students you can accept, rarely embracing experiential knowledge or contextual realities, without 'proving' equivalence to the accepted 'academic' benchmarks;

» academic regulations, the framework which seeks to guard and protect academic integrity, based on an implicit sector norm that seeks to replicate and constrain creativity;

» validation criteria, the point of scrutiny where those asking the questions (internal and external) are already the products of an existing, power-laden system.

In response to these, we replicate rather than reimagine, we ask previous students to contribute – knowing they are the product of a previous system, and we rarely reform or reconsider the curriculum in its entirety, as that would also question our identity and purpose. In revalidation, we seek the views of employers and students, to reflect 'what is now' rather than 'what will be' in four years, when our first graduates emerge. We might add an option module, to address a local or contemporary issue, not really believing it will be a constant, and we update our bibliography and reading lists to show we are current in our thinking.

Recent debates have at least challenged the white, middle-class guardians of knowledge and expertise to consider the breadth of their 'givens' – a challenge to decolonise the curriculum, and an emerging narrative that seeks to question the hierarchy of knowledge. Similarly, the recent global pandemic has required teacher and student to reconsider how they teach and learn, as we respond to the online pivot – for many academics, they have less knowledge and experience of this online world, and have needed to at least begrudgingly accept their students may bring some knowledge to the teacher–learner relationship.

To move beyond the minor changes we might make to broaden a reading list, or offer a more inclusive model of assessment to reflect diversity in all its forms, what fundamentally is needed is a new model of curriculum development. Not one that ignores the established frameworks, but instead uses them to enhance and develop the curriculum, rather than merely replicating it.

In an attempt to offer an alternative curriculum model, we have tried to reimagine the factors which currently 'limit' a creative and empowering model of curriculum, and view these as opportunities and guides, rather than a straitjacket.

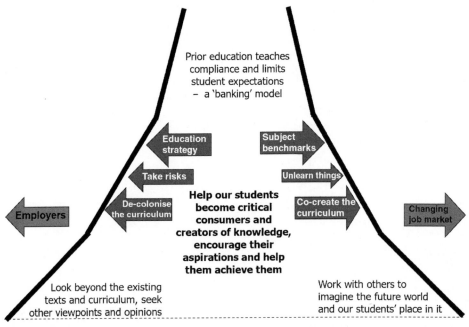

Figure 2.2 A reimagined and empowering model of curriculum.

In the model shown in Figure 2.2, we must still acknowledge that the prior experience of students is informed by a more traditional, 'banking' model of education, but instead of seeing this as limiting student expectations of higher education, we must help them 'unlearn' these things and work with them to shape a meaningful and contemporary curriculum. Students, no longer the passive consumer of 'our' collective and historical knowledge, but participants, critically engaged in shaping their knowledge and curriculum. Such a model seeks to draw attention to the limitations of their prior learning, asking them to take risks and look beyond the existing texts and curriculum.

You will see this model doesn't have the implicit 'scaffolding' that seeks to constrain learning; instead it aims to push boundaries, and co-create the curriculum through sharing viewpoints and opinions, valuing an individual's knowledge and life experiences. But to do this requires a significant reframing of higher education, a willingness to seek creative and untested ideas, rooted in critical pedagogy and underpinned by effective and robust quality assurance.

Critical issues

Wholescale reform of the curriculum

Using the metaphor of scaffolding, and the need to 'unlearn' the constraints of education and curriculum, Mike and Alan both draw on their experience of being youth and community workers, as well as teaching youth and community work. As a profession, it is rooted in education but represents a model of education that is shaped and informed by lived experience, conversation and democracy.

The challenge faced in trying to move towards a reimagined and empowering model of curriculum is that it is highly likely the 'guardians' of your academic standards – quality assurance teams, validation panels and even the Quality Assurance Agency Benchmark Statements – are informed by prior experience gained through a constraining curriculum, where prior knowledge and experience may limit their ability to think more creatively. In these examples, you are likely to hear people make reference to their experience as a student, their 'benchmark' of quality from a previous validation or a previous institution, their colonised and limiting set of curriculum resources and reference points.

We must all ask ourselves, how do we stop our previous experience from limiting future development and change, embracing and valuing different ideas and opinions?

Certainly in youth and community work, the biggest challenge was trying to find a set of words that reflected the language and ideas of curriculum, while embracing the values and ideals of informal education. This was eventually developed as a continuum, which reflected the democratic nature of the youth work process and the importance of dialogue and conversation as a means of sharing power. An adaptation of this might best be represented as in Figure 2.3.

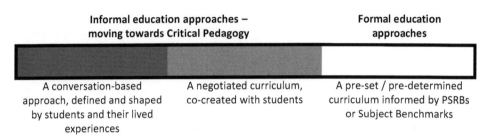

Figure 2.3 Towards a negotiated curriculum.

Adapted from Jeffs and Smith (1999).

Such a model recognises the importance of conversation and negotiation – 'working with' the students, rather than 'doing to' them. The significance of moving towards a negotiated curriculum has been reinforced in the latest iteration of the Youth Work Curriculum (National Youth Academy, 2020), where the emphasis is placed on the value of relationships and starting where the young person is at, in the National Youth Agency's refreshed curriculum – it places young people at its core, around which it wraps its four overarching principles: that it should be empowering, encourage participation (including in the decision-making), it should always seek to challenge inequality and promote equality and justice, and finally, the ultimate aim is educative.

Using the lessons from our shared experiences as youth and community workers, and reimagining our emerging models of curriculum, we are drawn to the latest iteration of the Youth Work Curriculum. As with Jeffs and Smith's (1999) negotiated curriculum, the National Youth Agency has tried to retain the language of curriculum, but instead of seeing it as limiting or a 'tick-box' exercise, they have completely reframed it, placing young people at the heart of the process. As seen in Figure 2.4, the relationship with the young person/people is rooted within the 'four pillars' which have defined youth work for nearly 50 years, and these are shaped by the values and ethics of our practice, which in turn is informed by, and informs, both theory and practice.

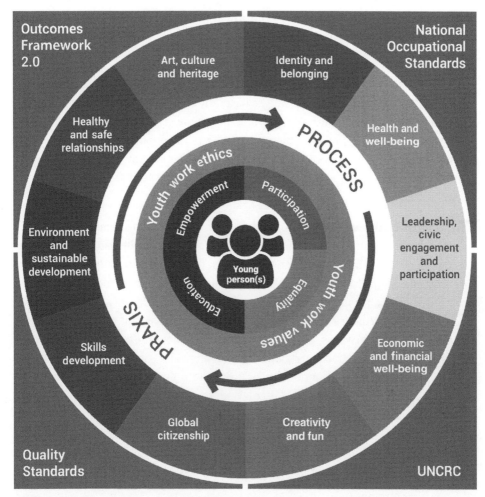

Figure 2.4 The NYA Curriculum Framework (2020).

Jeffs and Smith (1999), Youth Work Curriculum 2020 – NYA.

Wrapped around the four 'pillars' are the values and ethics which define and underpin our profession, but these can't exist in a vacuum and instead are used to inform both the process of youth work and our theory-informed practice/practice-informed theory (praxis). At this point, it could be claimed that youth work is finally moving towards critical pedagogy, but here is also the point at which we must recognise the external frameworks and realities in which we must exist, the terrain of our 'curriculum' (the outer ring); the contexts and locations in which our practice takes place, and which are shaped and informed by external factors and benchmarks that are recognised and valued by others.

This new NYA Curriculum Framework (National Youth Academy, 2020) provides us with a model that puts the learner at the centre, but even now it has generated various critiques which generally suggest that any framework must in itself impose order, power and limit choice and freedom. For some critics, the very fact that the outer ring has topics, titles or subjects creates a tension; but if we see them as an overlay, which can be replaced with ten other topics defined by context, location or contemporary debates, then a more fluid and ultimately less restrictive curricula document can emerge.

Were we to take this model and apply it to a Curriculum for Critical Pedagogy, our learners would be at the centre, our overarching principles might also include education, empowerment and equality; but instead of participation we could add autonomy, creativity and critical thinking. With such a model, placing the learner at the centre, surrounded by the principles of critical pedagogy, the next 'ring' would be theory/ practice – practice/theory, and here you could apply the central tenets of a subject discipline. Moving outwards, you could demonstrate how these could be delivered through a more negotiated curriculum where the outer ring becomes the broad module themes (we may even need several rings to reflect the levelness of learning and the scaffolding of subject knowledge). With this model, praxis, conversation and the learner are at the centre, rather than a didactic model of lecturing to passive recipients where the centre is existing knowledge. This model could potentially reshape the curriculum without undermining any of the established quality marks or academic integrity of higher education (the four outside corners, in this instance).

Conclusion

In higher education we consider research that is new, challenging and creating new knowledge as a benchmark for success, and yet we have an opposing view about teaching – we look 'backwards' to what we already know, unquestioned and unchallenged. Recent attention on the voices which dominate our curriculum – those white, middle-class and privileged demi-gods that we all quoted verbatim – are being reimagined, and the combined efforts of Student Unions, academics and authors are seeking to decolonise the curriculum, question the heteronormative assumptions and ultimately give voice to all.

The National Youth Agency, host of the Professional, Statutory and Regulatory Body for Youth and Community Work qualifications, ensures students have an equal voice in the discussions about education and training for future workers: the committee has a number of elected student representatives who can, and do, take a full and active part in the validation of courses. They contribute to the questioning of all parties, senior managers, lecturers, employers and students and participate in agreeing the final outcome and approval decision. Imagine a senior manager being held to account by a panel member, asking them to confirm their ongoing institutional commitment – and how much more powerful that question is when the person asking is a student from a different institution, someone for whom the institutional commitment impacts on their everyday experiences and future success.

Alan recently attended a validation event: that point of scrutiny where peers, critical friends and quality assurance colleagues seek to ensure the suitability and integrity of a new degree. Right at the end of the panel's conversation with the course development team was a question that embraced the challenge we all face when seeking to question the constraints of existing curriculum planning, and the way it replicates rather than revolutionises a subject discipline – a small movement away from the usual bibliographies and reading lists, but for Alan, very significant. The panel asked the team to discuss whether they felt the range of sources used, both in the design of the curriculum and the indicative module reading lists, reflected the diversity of their student group and was sufficiently inclusive to reflect university best practice? In framing this final section of the discussion, it allowed the team to show how they were moving beyond existing texts and curriculum, and working with others to imagine the future world our students will be engaging with.

Critical questions for practice

» How much of your current curriculum is shaped by your own experience of learning, and a historical view of the subject – and how much is looking beyond?

» How do you decide what 'goes in' your curriculum offer, and what is an 'option' or omitted – which voices become silenced?

» Is your current curriculum document more focused on the 'product' or the process of learning?

» How reflective and representative of your student cohort are the sources you use to shape the course and its curriculum, as well as the texts chosen as indicative reading?

Summary

- Curriculum does not need to be a straitjacket, which limits the opportunity to enact critical pedagogy. Each module can be reimagined, and re-considered, through conversation with students and peers such that it embraces creativity and opportunity for change.

- We can see co-creation of and in the curriculum as a starting point for developing our pedagogy and practices, as we move away from a product-led curriculum towards curriculum as praxis.

- A starting point for enacting critical pedagogy in the curriculum is to recognise that we must question what we already know and assume, just as we must ask our students to unlearn their experience of education and learning – enabling them to become critical consumers of knowledge, rather than merely replicating it.

Useful texts

Bovill, C and Woolmer, C (2019) How Conceptualisations of Curriculum in Higher Education Influence Student Staff Co-Creation in and of the Curriculum. *Higher Education*, 78: 407–22.

This article identifies four theoretical frameworks for conceptualising curriculum within higher education, acknowledging the traditions and values of critical pedagogy, as well as the challenges it can face within higher education. The authors offer differing perspectives as scholar and student and together explore and examine recognised curriculum theories and frameworks, before asking the reader to question some of their long-held beliefs about how we can work together to co-create curriculum in our everyday teaching and learning.

Costandius, E and Blitzer, E (eds) (2015) Curriculum Challenges in Higher Education. *Engaging Higher Education Curricula* (pp 9–26). Stellenbosch: SUN Press.

This introductory chapter provides an historical account of the role higher education could play in overcoming the challenges faced in South Africa as it embraced a new African democracy. It charts the desire to see education as empowering, and a way to embrace new freedoms and new energy for change. The authors see the significance of student and lecturer shaping the new curriculum, such that it supports economic and cultural change and promotes 'critical citizenship'.

Ord, J (2008) A Curriculum for Youth Work: The Experience of the English Youth Service. *Youth Studies Australia*, 27: 4.

This article charts the development and challenges faced by youth services in England as they tried to enact a curriculum that remained focused on the process of learning as opposed to some predetermined product or outcome. It acknowledges the external factors which might seek to impose or control the curriculum, while celebrating the inherent challenges of maintaining a young-person-centred model of practice. In doing so, it offers several ways to define curriculum: as content, product and process, not seeing them as mutually exclusive, but as interrelated and context-specific.

Chapter 3 | Critical pedagogy and assessment

Introduction

(Can) methods of authentic teaching and learning that deliberately subvert the conventional student and teacher relationship, that deconstruct the formal educational environment and curriculum and that invite students to question the standard modes and tropes of formal learning be combined with demands for clear learning outcomes and recognised forms of assessment required by university quality assurance processes.

(Serrano et al, 2018, p 12)

As Serrano indicates above, assessment in higher education can be seen as one of the most reductive elements of higher education. Certainly, many critical pedagogues and critical educators see it as the antithesis of authentic and critical learning. Smith below typifies and crystalises many critiques of summative assessment in higher education.

It is discriminatory, and it stigmatizes and disempowers individuals for life. It doesn't encourage anyone to read, write, learn, or think, though it does leave students and teachers frustrated, confused, despondent, resentful, and angry. I don't think assessment has any redeeming features, but, if it has, we are paying an exorbitant price for them. Assessment spawns difficulties faster than they can be dealt with. We don't need more tests or better tests; we need to extricate ourselves from tests.

(1995, p 587)

As Kahl (2013) discusses, assessments do not determine how well the students can *'analyze, interpret, and critique ideas'* (p 2612); instead, they often simply measure the degree to which students have memorised and can regurgitate the information that lecturers have decided signify them having 'learnt'. As Freire himself expressed it, talking about formal education and banking forms of education, assessment colonially is more about how well students have internalised the *'gift bestowed by those who consider themselves knowledgeable upon those whom they consider to know nothing'* (Freire, 1968, p 53). To illustrate, when Mike brought in some student self-determining techniques of critical pedagogy, a colleague countered *'but what if they do not want to learn the things that I know they need to?'*

Assessment is also in danger of framing the whole learning experience (Kahl, 2013; Serrano et al, 2018). Students are required to regurgitate pre-determined information derived from pre-set learning outcomes to symbolically represent their learning; this is derived from pre-set learning outcomes. We then teach to this assessment, rarely the subject, spelling out how they can reproduce what we require in order to get the best 'grade', which then again symbolises them having 'learnt' something. Concurrently, neither lecturer nor student is likely to express it as this cynical dynamic. Both parties know they are bound by, and consistently need to name check, words like 'critique', 'analysis', 'reflection' and 'reflexivity' that are prevalent in learning outcomes.

Pegg and Carr (2010), employing Bourdieu's (1998) concept of illusion, explore ways in which the learner, and we would argue by extension the educator, adapt to the 'rules-of-the-game', engaging in a duplicitous performance of a belief in 'learning for its own sake' and the 'importance of critique and reflection', while simultaneously calculating how to get the optimum grades, a part of which is espousing their love of learning and critique. Similarly, Trelfa (2016) talks about how reflection and reflective practice has itself become a performance, and at worst an elaborate form of self-justification.

The origins of assessment in education are interesting. The ancient Greeks used assessments as formative and not evaluative learning tools. Perhaps most tellingly, William Farish, a tutor at Cambridge University in England in 1792, came up with a method of teaching which would allow him to process more students in a shorter period of time. He invented grades (Hartmann, 2000). This grading system had originated earlier in the factories as a way of determining if the shoes made on the assembly line were 'up to grade', which in turn determined whether the workers should be paid and if the shoes could be sold (Hartmann, 2005). Transferring this to academia, William Farish found grading lessened his workload and reduced the hours he needed to spend in the classroom (Hartmann, 2005). He no longer needed to spend time assessing and evaluating individual students' minds to know if they understood a topic: his grading system did it for him and could be generalised across all students.

With summative assessment, fairness in assessment is normally argued for through standardisation, ie it is fair because everyone is asked the same thing. For a critical pedagogue, assessment is subjective, contextual and multilayered. Standardisation ignores all nuance, contextuality and subjectivity. Standardisation also ignores that the criteria of a standardised assessment will privilege a certain form of learning, and often a certain type of learner, ie the learning style and understandings of the dominant elite, as Barros illuminates:

Proponents of traditional forms of assessment assume that students can be tested fairly, in uniform ways, thus disregarding issues of socioeconomic dominance and cultural subordination that are intrinsically tied to any process of learning.

(2011, p 79)

Uniformity makes for economies of scale; if you can test 10 you can test 1000 – and do it a lot more quickly and cheaply. Hartmann (2005) also notes that adoption of uniform testing in turn transformed the classroom in that '*the lecture-hall/classroom shifted from a place where one heard the occasional speech by a famous thinker to the place of ordinary daily instruction*' (Hartmann, 2005).

Critical issues

Should critical pedagogy abandon the notion of assessment altogether?

Should a critical pedagogue go for a wholesale rejection of assessment? Several authors question this (Kahl, 2013; Keesing-Styles, 2003) saying that while rejected by many critical pedagogues, assessment is a necessary part of education, because it helps both students and lecturers determine how well all parties are learning and understanding things. Developing generative themes and critical consciousness are complex, difficult processes that are by definition counter-intuitive. Without any criteria to measure whether our themes are truly generative, and whether we are achieving conscientisation, we may be simply reinscribing the dominant hegemony. These processes cannot remain unexamined, unchecked and left to chance.

Making assessment compatible with critical pedagogy

Kahl (2013) argues that assessment can be a positive tool and can work towards the critical pedagogy goal of conscientisation. He thought it was possible to come up with processes for '*determining whether students are developing a heightened awareness of hegemony, identifying avenues for praxis, and developing means to respond to hegemony when they discern its presence in society*' (2013, p 2610). Others such as Shor thought we need to be rigorous about assessment, and that our approach to it needs to be steeped in critical pedagogy:

the instruments used to test and measure students should be based in a student-centred, co-operative curriculum. This means emphasizing narrative grading, portfolio assessments, group projects and performances, individual exhibitions, and essay examinations that promote critical thinking instead of standardized or short-answer tests.

(Shor, 1992, p 144)

Freire himself was not against assessment per se but opposed assessment that does not provide students with '*opportunities to consciously develop a critical framework in which they confront the validity of their acquired evaluative system against other systems*' (Barros, 2011, p 83). Freire (1996) recognised the negative effect neoliberalism has had on what assessment has become, arguing that the dominant class in society hides their subjectivity and ideology within calls for objective, 'neutral' assessment and technical training over critical learning. Neoliberal ideology furthers the banking model of education and lends itself to assessment procedures that reinscribe this hegemony in the name of neutrality.

Therefore, for Freire, modern assessment processes have become antithetical to a critical agenda, but this is not something inherent in assessment conceptually, but how it has been operationalised and used by the dominating elites. In this hegemonic system, students are not afforded the opportunity to critique knowledge or examine society's impact on their lives. Rather, as Giroux says:

assessment prepares students for corporate life. Thus, students are not challenged to think critically about corporations' role in promoting injustice in society, but instead are taught to view knowledge as capital – something to be used only to gain profit for the individual.

(Giroux, 2005, p 43)

Standardisation is one of the expressions of this dominant ideology of assessment – however, what is the critical pedagogic alternative?

Kahl (2013) favours autoethnographic approaches and suggests criteria to assess reflective writing based on Engstrom's (2008) five general principles of autoethnographic writing:

1   critically reflecting upon prejudices that the student brings to the situation;

2   examining the effect that the student has on the marginalised group;

3   evaluating the role of ethics in the student's writing and interactions with the marginalised;

4   discussing the impact that the student's writing has on himself/herself and the marginalised group;

5   reflecting on what the student has learned about power in society through his/her interactions with the marginalised group.

For students we would substitute lecturer and student, or indeed participants, which can include others outside of the institution, who are nevertheless part of the learning experience, including family friends, communities and all the other people within and linked to the university. The depth of the student's understanding and application of the concept should be assessed – the question is what is assessed, by whom and how this is determined.

Characteristics of authentic assessment within critical pedagogy

Keesing-Styles (2003) identifies a number of characteristics of what an authentic critical pedagogic approach to assessment might look like. We have given examples for each characteristic.

It should be centred on dialogic interactions so that the roles of teacher and learner are shared and all voices are validated

Many students have not considered that they are knowledge creators before. One assessment Mike has used at both foundation and master's level is to get the student to come up with their own theories on something, and then defend them to a group. This has led to some very interesting ideas, and in-depth analysis – it also gets students to fundamentally question who gets to create knowledge and be heard. Another set of questions could consider what roles are being played out in the room, ie what is the role of a lecturer, a student, a mature student and what performances are being played out in the classroom? What are our perceptions of each other and what our jobs entail – what other roles do we perform as people and what bearing does that have on the learning situation? Exploring such phenomena will fit criteria for assessment, such as undertaking research, analytic application, data collection, linking and developing concepts, etc – typical things within assessment criteria.

Example 3.1

Exploring knowledge and learning in the classroom

Relevant principles: *knowledge should relate to the lived experience of participants.*

Relevant aims: *to develop critical thinkers who create new knowledge.*

Relevant approaches: *emphasising the importance of democracy and equality in learning environments.*

As a portfolio question, Mike has asked students to consider '*who is learning what in the lecturer/student relationship*'. This can include questions such as: who is learning at this moment and how? What is the lecturer learning and how? What is the student learning and how? What learning happens for the university? What learning happens within other relationships we are all involved in? The last one often causes the most debate as one considers ways one has learnt to do things in the past and how transferable this is. There are deeper questions: who creates knowledge, and who gets heard when there are competing versions of knowledge and what is true? Getting them to explore the common characteristics of who is heard inevitably reveals that knowledge creators are often hegemonic males, pale, neurotypical and from certain class backgrounds – this is often a revelation to students who may think knowledge creation is neutral.

Foster an integrated approach to theory and practice, or what Freire would term praxis – theory in action

Kahl (2013) identified what assessment in critical pedagogy should achieve. It should heighten awareness of hegemony in the classroom and in society, identify avenues for praxis and take steps towards praxis. While quite a tall order, this is not an impossible to ask.

Example 3.2

Assessing praxis

Relevant principles: *knowledge should relate to the lived experience of participants. Education is inherently political. Knowledge should be co-created between all participants in the learning process.*

Relevant aims: *to develop critical thinkers who create new knowledge. For people to become aware of their, and others', oppressions. For people to make connections between personal experiences and wider societal forces.*

$\longrightarrow$

> **Relevant approaches:** *emphasising a co-created flexible curriculum using authentic materials, generative themes and finding teachable moments.*
>
> In a module on trade union education, the group assessment followed the process for developing generative themes. Firstly, the group explored what interests and issues they had in common. They then had to examine the wider societal issues, tensions and contradictions behind these issues. They then had to come up with not only a plan of action, looking at power and influence around the issues, but also identifying what agency they had in the situations and what meaningful impact they could have. For some it was linked to placement so that they could actually undertake the action and make a real-world impact.

Recent union action had largely been around paid settlements and lecturers' working conditions. It was recognised that, to some degree, this was alienating students who were understandably worried about their education being disrupted. The students developed a series of actions to educate other union members and other students about the general state of higher education and seek common ground between parties. Actions and teachable moments were sought on the picket lines and beyond. Discussions were held about the pressures that are put on both lecturers and students, both financially and in terms of workload, leading to Student Union support of the disputes.

This has led to a discussion about how education is being commodified and stratified and reduced to training for employment. In turn this led to students boycotting new government 'quality regimes' that were reductive. An integral part of the assessment was a reflection on the process, including an analysis of the power dynamics within the student group, staff, the local community and the wider campaign – particularly in how they treated each other, and were involved in the empowerment of the local population.

It should value and validate the experience students bring to the classroom

Example 3.3

Acknowledging the knowledge in the room

Relevant principles: *knowledge should be co-created between all participants in the learning process.*

Relevant aims: *to develop critical thinkers who create new knowledge.*

Relevant approaches: *emphasising the importance of democracy and equality in learning environments.*

A simple way that Mike has incorporated acknowledging the knowledge in the room when they look at a topic, any topic is that they must first explore who in the room has knowledge on it, and this includes the lecturer, all students, in the wider institution, in the wider community and in the space in between. The students then explore the quality of this information, and perhaps as importantly, who is judging the quality of this information and how. Plenty of academic criteria can be applied to assess this, preferably developed with the students themselves, including how many sources are identified, the depth of analysis, lateral thinking, making connections, etc.

Reinterpret the complex ecology of relationships in the classroom to avoid oppressive power relations

Such questions make for some fascinating discussions, particularly as initially students feel powerless, and also project onto the lecturer many things that are actually institutional power, such as devising courses and passing people. It can also be a space to problem pose, such as what would happen if the students collectively decided to walk out, or all not do an assessment? A further problem Mike has posed is looking at who has power and influence in the university – asking students to look through different websites and documentation to explore the power structure, who sits on the senate, who's on the exam board, the committee structure of the course, etc. A worked example could be how they could get an issue raised – and what they could do if they did not like the response. More widely, Kahl (2013) discusses how we could explore with students the depth of their understanding of hegemony with such questions as *'how do you believe that hegemony functions in society?' 'Have your views of covert power in society changed since learning about this concept?' 'How have your views changed?'*

Example 3.4

Assessing who has power in the room (or not!)

Relevant principles: *education is inherently political.*

⟶

Relevant aims: *for people to become aware of their, and others', oppressions. For people to make connections between personal experiences and wider societal forces.*

Relevant approaches: *emphasising the importance of democracy and equality in learning environments.*

Another portfolio question has asked students to consider who has power in the room. What power does the lecturer have, both in the room and outside of it, in relation to the student and the university? What power does the institution have in these relationships? (and what do we mean by the institution?). What power does the student have, both in the room, in relationship to other students and the lecturer and to the university?

Create a negotiated curriculum, including assessment, equally owned by teachers and students

This area is perhaps the most important. The above assessments are all ones that could be done without the involvement of students in their design yet would be much richer and closer to the spirit of critical pedagogy if they were. We mentioned the self-censoring tendencies of many academics in the curriculum chapter, cries of 'quality wouldn't allow us to do that' from people who have not actually spoken to quality about it. In the aforementioned critical pedagogy modules, students had free rein to come up with the module learning outcomes, and then to design its assessment, including, as it often did, students being either intimately involved in that assessment, or even taking a lead on it.

One of the difficulties on any course is that of attendance and the related issue of participation. People may turn up, but do they participate? Building on work conducted at Cardiff Metropolitan University, Newman co-produced a matrix looking at criteria for participation including: integration of theory and practice into classroom; interaction, participation and reflection in action; demonstration of professional attitude and demeanour and attendance. At level 4 this was assessed by the tutor, at level 5 it was co-produced, at level 6 students assessed each other, with tutors moderating. In the eight years this has been used the students have always taken it seriously and behaved professionally. Memorably defending the approach at the validation event, a student panel countered concerns that students would set up 'kangaroo courts' against each other by asking why the panel had such little faith in them, but also why their kangaroo courts would be any worse that the existing one of tutors – and theirs would have a lot more transparency and accountability.

Example 3.5

Involving students in designing and undertaking assessment

Relevant principles: *knowledge should be co-created between all participants in the learning process.*

Relevant aims: *to develop critical thinkers who create new knowledge.*

Relevant approaches: *emphasising the importance of democracy and equality in learning environments. Emphasising a co-created flexible curriculum using authentic materials, generative themes and finding teachable moments.*

Alan has enacted self and peer marking in one of his modules. This task is worth 40 per cent of the overall module mark and following feedback from students on group-based assessments, a maximum of 10 per cent of the overall group mark is awarded based on an individual's contribution to the process and presentation. This means that if your overall assessment mark was 65 per cent, everyone will get 55 per cent but up to an additional 10 per cent can be awarded based on an individual's contribution to the planning and delivery. Group members evaluate their own contribution and the contribution of group members to the fulfilment of the assessment task.

A colleague of Alan's has written a chapter on their experience of working within a module trying to enact critical pedagogy where he was not able to have such influence:

Typically, in universities, most aspects of module design (including assessments) are specified months before courses run. However, within the quality assurance system at Leeds Beckett University, there is no requirement for weightings of portfolio components to be specified in advance. Therefore, the group discussed how this presented an opportunity to agree democratically what percentage of overall marks would be constituted by each of the three portfolio components.

(Muskett, 2017, p 220)

As a true critical pedagogue, he was not only acknowledging the limiting factors of the system and assessment, but was also trying to get the most integrity out of it as possible.

Critical issues

Can critical pedagogy be used in non-education-based modules, including STEM?

The question arises of whether Keesing-Styles' (2003) criteria and Kahl's (2013) taxonomy are achievable within non-education-based modules? Mike ran a session with foundation year practitioners, and they discussed whether it was possible to undertake critical pedagogy within STEM subjects. Interestingly lots of examples were given of how this was possible, including how this could be assessed. Environmental science gave examples of very similar processes of developing generative themes and engaging with the political processes of scientific knowledge creation. A mathematics lecturer ran sessions on 'everyday mathematics' looking at how people did or did not use mathematics in everyday life, from people in poverty, counting up the cost of their shopping basket as they went along, to people who wanted to get drunk as quickly and cheaply as possible doing four-way mathematical equations on prices by volume, by alcoholic content, recognising that an effervescent drink of 20 per cent alcoholic content is the optimum 'balance' to get alcohol into one's bloodstream the quickest.

On the aforementioned foundation course, there was an element of statistics. The assessment explored how statistics, and more generally research, was used to privilege certain positions, and how making quantitative research 'elite knowledge' re-enforces this. Students had to investigate certain statistical claims and evaluate them, including what power was being exercised. Students reported getting past their own 'mathematics freeze', locating this avoidance in the way that they had been historically taught mathematics and how it had been constructed, which then opened them up to engage with other STEM subjects that they had previously found alienating.

Conclusion

Critical pedagogy and assessment are potentially compatible, particularly if we take assessment's original conceptualisation as being able to ensure that learning has taken place – indeed on this level it is essential. Indeed, we have argued elsewhere that avoidance of assessment, particularly self-assessment, can lead to the defence of bad practice, sloppy analysis and not the development of critical consciousness (Seal, 2019). Much formative assessment in higher education is a compromise and is framed in a neoliberal context that seeks to reduce and individualise it and ignore the forms of knowledge and learning that it privileges in purporting to be neutral.

However, to reject assessment outright is to not engage with the real world of higher education, and, as Alinsky (1989) would have put it, to indulge in highly principled but unaccountable failure. Critical pedagogy is about engaging with the real world, which is also dominated by neoliberal and neo-conservative thinking. We need to work the system for maximum integrity and work out which compromises are worth taking and which are not – we think assessment has enough potential that we should engage with it – for now.

Critical questions for practice

» Have you ever rejected assessment outright – without it how do you know learning has taken place and whether critical consciousness has been achieved?

» Have you ever been guilty of saying that quality assurance processes, or other structures framing courses, would not allow us to do something without checking out if this is actually the case?

» How could you build into assessment an exploration of power in the classroom, the nature of learning, who has knowledge in the room, who creates knowledge and how this links to wider institutional and societal issues?

» How could you meaningfully involve the student in the design and execution of assessment on your courses?

Summary

- Assessment is generally rejected by critical pedagogues as being reductive, individualised, inaccurate and creating divisions between students and students and students and lecturers.

- However, assessment, in its original form of examining whether and what learning has taken place, has an essential role in terms of accountability for critical pedagogues if we are working towards people developing critical consciousnesses.

- There are plenty of examples of how assessment can be done within a critical pedagogic framework, including the all-important step of involving students in designing and delivering assessment, and we have to find the most integrity we can within the system we operate within – a process that has parallels to the goals of critical pedagogy itself.

Useful texts

Kahl Jr, D H (2013) Critical Communication Pedagogy and Assessment: Reconciling Two Seemingly Incongruous Ideas. *International Journal of Communication*, 7: 21.

This article outlines how many critical educators struggle with the idea of assessment, viewing it as a practice that stifles a critical communication pedagogical agenda. However, Kahl argues that assessment is a necessary part of education, because it helps instructors to determine how well students are meeting course goals and can be a positive tool to help critical educators to work towards conscientisation. In turn it can determine whether students are developing a heightened awareness of hegemony, identifying avenues for praxis and developing means to respond to hegemony when they discern its presence in society. The article then provides examples of how critical educators can help students reach conscientisation.

Keesing-Styles, L (2003). The Relationship between Critical Pedagogy and Assessment in Teacher Education. *Radical Pedagogy*, 5(1): 1–19.

The article begins by examining how critical pedagogy has evolved over the years and what critiques are inherent within it or have been directed towards it, particularly in how it has been enacted in higher education. The article then focuses on the issue of assessment, particularly in teacher education, and the possibility of incorporating some of the principles and practices of critical pedagogy in the assessment process in this setting. The work of several writers is considered in relation to the establishment of empowering processes, not only for learning, but also for assessment.

Muskett T A (2017) Popular Education in Practice: A Case Study of Radical Educational Praxis in a Contemporary UK University. In Seal, M (ed) *Trade Union Education: Transforming the World* (pp 216–27). Oxford: New Internationalist.

This chapter is about a group of students and a lecturer undertaking a module 'Critical Psychology in Practice', offered to students on an undergraduate psychology degree in the UK, which was explicitly designed and delivered using democratic and community-based teaching and learning methods, including critical pedagogy. In this chapter, they historically and politically situate the module in relation to the modern UK university, describe how critical pedagogy informed the process of teaching and learning on this course and explore some of the complexities associated with its implementation.

Introduction

Overall, there seems to be a general openness to critical pedagogy. Therefore, teachers may need to carefully consider the socio-political conditions they are in, because this pedagogy could potentially disrupt order and harmony in the classroom.

(Jeyaraj, 2020, p 434)

As we have already seen, there is a natural hesitance in adopting critical pedagogic approaches, and this includes teaching and learning – whether that is our fear as the teacher, or students' reluctance to embrace it – or whether it is the implicit power relationships that exist within higher education, and the subtle but all-consuming power of neoliberalism and the feeling from many students that they have paid for their education, and want to be 'taught'. However, as Jeyaraj expresses above, there is also an appetite and enthusiasm for it, particularly once it has been experienced.

Critical issues

Covid-19, blended learning and critical pedagogy

We have heard many colleagues who adhere to critical pedagogy say that it is not possible online and that we need that visceral experience of being in front of someone for it to be genuine and authentic. However, it looks like the old model of everything being face to face is becoming redundant as we explored in Chapter 1 – does this in turn mean that critical pedagogy is redundant, or not possible? We would argue not.

For those of us who have lived through the challenges and changes to higher education during the global pandemic, so much has changed that could help address the power imbalances within the classroom, and higher education in general. Students have seen lecturers delivering classes from their own homes, removing the power imbalance that can so easily manifest in a classroom or lecture theatre. In the early days, as the online pivot occurred, many lecturers relied on the students to navigate the online world – whether it was asking about screen-sharing, or the best platform to share video content.

We have all been more open, the screen has required new skills and given new insights, but it has also created a blurring between the conventions of hierarchical communication and our social connectedness. Using a mobile phone to respond to an email, it is easy to slip into text speak, and the desire to add an emoji can be overwhelming! But Covid-19 has created other challenges: how do you welcome and inculcate a course value base into a virtual induction? What can you do to establish the cultural norms and practices of the course or university? Alan's students worked with staff to co-produce a good practice guide for staff and students about teaching in the new reality – all about expectations, etiquette and behaviours, which started to address what blended and online teaching informed by critical pedagogy could look like.

Giroux, who has perhaps written the most extensively on critical pedagogy and higher education, also offers some pointers to what is crucial within pedagogic spaces, with creating a spirit of questioning being foregrounded.

Educators need to consider defining pedagogy, if not education itself, as central to producing those democratic public spheres that foster an informed citizenry. Pedagogically, this points to modes of teaching and learning capable of enacting and sustaining a culture of questioning, and enabling the advancement of what Kristen Case calls 'moments of classroom grace'.

(Giroux, 2017, p 90)

He further articulates:

Moments of grace in this context are understood as moments that enable a classroom to become a place to think critically, ask troubling questions and take risks, even though that may mean transgressing established norms and bureaucratic procedures. Pedagogies of classroom grace should provide the conditions for students and others to reflect critically on commonsense understandings of the world and begin to question their own sense of agency, relationships to others, and relationships to the larger world.

(Giroux, 2017, p 90)

We need to rethink how our evolving universities, however pedagogy is enacted and structured, can cultivate, sustain and maintain these moments of grace.

This chapter offers four ways that the teaching and learning experience can be delivered honouring critical pedagogic principles: questioning our existing approaches by deconstructing the lecture; questioning who gets to teach and has expertise in the room; re-defining tutor groups and the idea of self-directed learning; and re-articulating the academic conference or seminar.

De-constructing the lecture

Freire (1970a) famously critiqued the lecture approach to teaching as being a banking model. In critiquing it, he articulated what a critical pedagogic approach might look like:

A 'tool for social and cultural emancipation', something that could be achieved through portraying and practising education as a political and pedagogical project in which dialogue, democratization of teacher–student relationships, co-construction of the curriculum and making learning relevant to the learner are valued.

(Freire, quoted in Schugurensky, 2014, p 39)

As Clark (2018, p 988) articulated '*Looking at HE from a Freirean perspective, it might be considered that the lecture does not fulfil any of the aims of critical pedagogy, or of a transformative HE more generally*'. He goes on to look at whether, as a form of teaching, it could have merit for critical pedagogues (not much he concludes). Tom Muskett, mentioned in the previous chapter with regard to working within the prescribed assessment, took this critique to the students.

Example 4.1

Critical pedagogy and scaffolding learning: the deconstruction of the lecture

Relevant principles: *education is inherently political.*

Relevant aims: *for people to make connections between personal experiences and wider societal forces.*

Relevant approaches: *emphasising the importance of democracy and equality in learning environments.*

Tom Muskett, a colleague of Alan's, recently delivered a presentation at a staff conference, alongside a group of students. All of them had participated in a first-year module from their psychology degree, but in the opening sessions of the module, Tom had asked the students why academics use lectures, and what the benefits were. In doing so, he was starting to prepare the students to become critical consumers of their education. A small step, but it created considerable debate and provided two clear messages about the nature of lectures.

First that they are ***educational:***

» the actual material itself (the **overt curriculum**);

» the skills and knowledge about *how to learn* the material – part of the **hidden curriculum.**

Second that they are ***social:***

» the lecture as a communal event which brings (like-minded?) people together;

» link to integration, preparation and orientation;

» experiences vary based on individual difference.

He then went on to introduce them to some of the key ideas of Paulo Freire, in particular the 'classed' nature of education philosophy, which imposes dominant ideals and in doing so reproduces oppression at multiple levels, and the 'banking' model of education that the students will previously have experienced.

Students were then encouraged to draw out the similarities between lectures and these characteristics of their previous education – one-way communication/presentation, passive recipients, ignoring their individual life experiences. In the presentation, one of the students felt able to say *'lecturers are familiar with **the** university experience, but **not** familiar with **OUR** university experience'*. Tom, using problem-solving techniques, encouraged the group to share how they wanted to enact critical pedagogy within their lectures, sharing the ownership and experience with each other, valuing discussion and debate, seeing learning as mutual – valuing lived experience in equal measure to others' knowledge. Having introduced students to critical pedagogy in their first year of study, even though this example focused on one element of their learning – the lecture (context) – it meant by their final year, they had embraced many of the key principles of critical pedagogy, and were ready to embrace and enact critical pedagogy at a modular level – not only that, but also to write it up as co-authors, with Tom!

The final-year module referred to in the example above, Critical Psychology in Practice, was an optional module that was shaped by students' lived experiences. Students considered the concepts of critical pedagogy when applied to their time at university, critiquing and questioning many of the neoliberal assumptions on which current education practice is based. Each three-hour session started with small groups sharing their lived experiences, on a theme they had identified the previous week: gender, family, mental health, etc. Gradually the discussion was broadened out to the whole group; people shared very personal accounts but never felt judged, and eventually individuals were asked to reflect on their lived experience in relation to power, education and society. There was space for 'content' but this was rarely delivered as a lecture; instead it 'emerged' through the contributions and conversations. Students also describe how learning went 'beyond the classroom' as they started to have these conversations with family and friends (Canham et al, 2017).

Respecting the knowledge in the room

Some years ago, Mike ran a module on intersectionality, building on a previous module on diversity. Student received weekly teaching on different 'aspects' of diversity, eg gender, race, sexuality and so on and wrote a generalised assignment at the end, looking at how diversity is important in their practice. At revalidation the team discussed how we found the diversity module inadequate in addressing the multiplicities of people's identities, that it gave insufficient attention to the issues of race and that it focused on the 'other', rather than looking at our own multiplicities and complicities.

Mike remembers standing in front of the group on the first day and seeing that the group was 60 per cent female and 80 per cent global majority, and admitting to them that he could not teach them. He could not stand there as a white middle-aged man and teach them about diversity: the knowledge and experience was in the room; it just needed unearthing, acknowledging and articulating. Example 4.2 outlines what Mike did.

Example 4.2

Reconstructing the teaching of diversity

Relevant principles: *knowledge should relate to the lived experience of participants. Education is inherently political.*

Relevant aims: *for people to become aware of their, and others', oppressions. For people to make connections between personal experiences and wider societal forces.*

Relevant approaches: *emphasising the importance of democracy and equality in learning environments. Emphasising a co-created flexible curriculum using authentic materials, generative themes and finding teachable moments.*

Mike presented his understanding of himself in terms of intersectionality and Kyriarchy (Fiorenza, 2009) and how this impacted on his practice. He talked about how on some levels he had experienced oppression in practice and higher education being dyslexic, working class and queer. Conversely, Mike is Cis Male, middle-aged and white, which brings a lot of privilege. Mike also discussed the non-neutrality of being a professor, which may well be a result of that privilege (given statistics on the lack of women and black professors), and what responsibility that then places on him. All this was about the critical pedagogic aim of breaking down barriers between the learner and learned and bringing personal experiences into the public domain. On the module he brought in a number of other lecturers, ex and current students, and practitioners to do similarly.

Mike introduced the ideas of Rancière (1991), explaining that he was not going to 'teach' them about intersectionality, but was adopting the role of an 'Ignorant Schoolmaster', his role being to help them articulate, conceptualise and contextualise their existing knowledge. It was agreed that Mike would act as a consultant to them in their development of resources on topics such as sexuality, race, gender, class and their intersections, which they would in turn present to others on how to work with these issues with young people and communities.

In the revalidation Mike recognised there were two halves to the module. The first half explicitly looked at the notion of the self within the context of the private and the public. Students were required to give an assessed presentation on themselves and how they understood their identities, acknowledging how they may be constructed by others, and how they mediated this. The second half consisted of students doing teaching sessions on various aspects of diversity and intersectionality, which was then co-assessed by the other students.

Tutor groups: flipping the flipped classroom

The idea of the flipped classroom has caused excitement lately; although we cannot see how it is vastly different from the idea that students should be reading prior to coming to the session, although the problem-solving approach has merit. A critical pedagogue would want to take this much further and have the student determine the contents of what is covered in the sessions. Self-directed tutor groups are one way of doing this.

Example 4.3

The self-directed tutor group

Relevant principles: *knowledge should relate to the lived experience of participants. Knowledge should be co-created between all participants in the learning process.*

Relevant aims: *to develop critical thinkers who create new knowledge. For people to become aware of their, and others', oppressions. For people to make connections between personal experiences and wider societal forces.*

Relevant approaches: *emphasising the importance of democracy and equality in learning environments. Emphasising a co-created flexible curriculum using authentic materials, generative themes and finding teachable moments.*

The foundation year at Newman University is aimed at 'non-traditional' undergraduate students and resists the dominant deficit discourse of undergraduate transition. The stated starting point was not that students have failed in the education system, but that the formal educational and/or societal structures and systems have failed them. Foundation years should thus seek to support the perpetual process of our students' becoming; the constantly dissolving, diffusing and recreation of their subjectivity that is engaged in a perpetual process of flux (Quinn, 2010, pp 18–22). Mediating and working through these experiences requires an approach that enables teaching staff to respond according to the needs of a student group in any given moment. The approach is influenced by a combination of the Swedish Folk High School Grundtvig model of education, critical pedagogy and Tavistock experiential group work.

A key feature of the approach is a three-hour student-led tutor group that is responsive to student need, rather than requiring delivery of predetermined, set content. Students determine the agenda of the meeting from the outset, the starting point being why and how this can happen, and why this different approach is being taken. Students often resist, which again becomes part of the discussion. Evaluations and student partnership work reveal that students see tutor groups as one of the transformative elements of the course that makes their experience coherent and provides a space for them to work through their previous and current constructions of themselves and their education. A student describes the experience:

Tutor group helped me understand my school's experience and see that someone like me could make a success of education, it made me quite angry really, but now I want to do something with that anger.

In an article cowritten with students, Seal and Parkes (2019, p 8) elaborate on the process:

Students discuss the notion of their 'possible selves' that are drawn from and relate to past and future representations of 'self'. These are marked by their own sociological, cultural and historical contexts (Markus and Nurius, 1986) that aids them in considering the socially constructed notions of identity and furthers reflection on their own 'becoming' within the context of the university. Through this process of deconstructing and reconstructing their experiences and understandings, the students and tutors create new knowledge about the nature of the world.

Tutor groups have a particular focus: deconstructing and reconstructing students' previous educational experiences to resist internalised deficit thinking and negotiate the resources students will need to traverse higher education; exploring, deconstructing and reconstructing concepts encountered on the course; creating active, mutual, knowledge-generating spaces, challenging more 'banking' models of education; and discussing the notion of student (and tutors) 'possible selves' that are drawn from and relate to past and future representations of 'self'.

The writers also thought that the tutor has a particular role within the group. Interestingly, many tutors found it really hard not to try and fill the space – having to learn to ride their own anxiety, and sometimes that of the students, and have faith that, left to their own devices the students would fill the space and take a lead. Many of them would come up with 'little exercises' in case students were quiet – it took a collective will to resist this falling back into old conventions. To try and counter these tendencies we tried to better articulate the role of a tutor. It is to: monitor the time-bound nature of the experience; keep the group on the task of examining a broad curriculum; facilitate the deconstruction of previous and current educational experiences and offer observations on group processes; act on the students' will, self-belief and efficacy, the will to engage and challenge themselves and others, and to wish to learn, encourage and affirm students' intrinsic ways of knowing as legitimate, but as perhaps needing to be tightened and articulated; aid students to understand and deconstruct both the language and concepts behind the arguments they use and to enable students to make connections (ie not make the connections for them) between their personal issues and wider social forces and vice-versa, exploring tensions and contradictions between the two.

As we will discuss in Chapter 6, these are not easy spaces. The evaluation found that tutor group spaces had particular characteristics: they may be visceral, pedagogic and liminal, rather than safe, though certainly not dangerous; they may have an emphasis on deconstructing power, both inside and outside of the space, and the concept of knowledge and its creation; they may have a process framework of inter-subjectivity, encounter, recognition and working in the moment and they may have an emphasis on cultivating hope and a future orientation, recognising an equal emphasis on reconstruction as on deconstruction.

Deconstructing the conference and the academic seminar

Interestingly, one of the aspects of pedagogy that is rarely questioned is how we engage each other in education. As we will explore more in Chapter 6, the academic conference and seminar have had a very set format. The rise of the poster presentation is more about fitting in more presentations than about its pedagogic potential. Approaches such as the unconference, Open Space Technology and, to a degree, World Café events have the potential to be far more compatible with critical pedagogy.

Example 4.4

Organising the unconference

Relevant principles: *knowledge should relate to the lived experience of participants. Knowledge should be co-created between all participants in the learning process.*

Relevant aims: *to develop critical thinkers who create new knowledge.*

Relevant approaches: *emphasising the importance of democracy and equality in learning environments. Emphasising a co-created flexible curriculum using authentic materials, generative themes and finding teachable moments. The importance of cultivating hope and symbolic resistance.*

In 2019 Mike was the co-organiser of an international staff week entitled 'University as Community: breaking the circle of certainty – students and staff working together'. Its pedagogic approach was based on 'open space technology' (Owen, 2008), an approach which Mike feels is compatible with critical pedagogy. Owen (2008) noticed that most of the effective learning in conferences happened in the informal spaces outside of, and around, the formal sessions. Consequently, the organising principle for this event is based on what happens in these spaces, rather than formal ones. Conference themes and sessions are developed over the course of the week, rather than being decided beforehand. People had to take responsibility for bringing ideas, for going through a democratic process to share those ideas and take collective responsibility for developing a vision for these themes to become realities. It was attended by over 50 people from 10 different countries and included support staff, students at all levels and academics. It lasted four days and culminated in an exhibition, presentation/performance for all staff including one of the Pro-Vice Chancellors.

There is also one rule: 'the rule of two feet'. It means participants were free to decide which session they wanted to attend and were able to switch to another one at any time. This might mean a session may have no one in it. It might give that person time to think through their issues for themselves. There are also certain characters that are named to enable movement. People can be bumblebees, who fly from group to group cross-pollinating the discussions, or butterflies who sit around looking relaxed – interesting discussions emerge around them as people find them and pause to chat. This means that people could leave and come together in more informal spaces and set up their own session. Open spaces are created where people can come together and do something different, as long as they take responsibility for feeding back what they discuss and agree. Networking can occur before, during, after and in between the actual face-to-face meetings so discussions can continue seamlessly.

Comments from participants at the unconference introduced above have been positive, indicating that the events did have an effect on how people saw their social realities and institutions. Quite what made it work is harder to identify. Perhaps the co-organiser, the international co-ordinator, sheds the best light on this:

What was particularly useful was the opportunity to rehearse working in a different way. It can be a big leap of faith to ask participants and organizers to hold such an open event. But the value is that each participant can practice using their voice, challenging power, being listened to and holding their power, listening and letting others lead. As we can see, stepping outside our comfort zone or questioning those we perceive to have more power than us can be difficult. As we experienced, there can be a lot of emotion involved in stepping into the unknown, so an opportunity for a trial performance can tell us a lot about ourselves and others.

(McLoughlin et al, 2021, p 224)

Having contacted participants subsequently, impacts have been:

> » a colleague went on to completely reorganise the conference they were responsible for later that year, and it was enthusiastically received and led to concrete change at a strategic level;

> » another colleague rewrote their communications strategy, changing the way that committees were organised in the institution;

> » another colleague wrote an institutional paper on the method, which they circulated to all colleagues, and have started using it in their teaching practice.

The Pro-Vice Chancellor commented:

We always talk about academic staff, support staff and students together, but this has given us a vision of how it is possible to put it into practice – I shall be taking this model back to the senior management team for serious consideration.

It became the organising principle of the next three teaching and learning conferences.

Conclusion

We have shared just a few examples. Once one embraces the principles of critical pedagogy, one's learning and teaching style will change accordingly and naturally. Of critical pedagogy's principles, perhaps the most important is about letting go of power and trusting that students will step into the breach and let their own knowledge flow. In a recent inaugural professorial lecture by Stella Jones-Davitt (www.youtube.com/watch?v=MMXaXDIHFJ8), she stressed the point that critical pedagogy was transformational not transactional, a theme which we hope this book demonstrates.

Of the pedagogic skills we need to develop, the most important seems to be able to react in the moment – to be able to look for teachable moments, to be able to work the room, mining people's ideas and linking them, and enabling students to make their own connections. Yet reflection in action (Schön, 1987) is very under theorised (Eraut, 2004; Harris and Seal, 2014); the ability to be able to respond authentically, effectively and pedagogically in the moment and take it to a developmental place is by no means easy and we have to learn to hone it as a skill. Harris (2014), coming from a jazz musician's background, calls it improvisation. Improvisation is not just making it up on the spot. It is about drawing on a vast vocabulary and applying it to the moment, and in that moment creating something new. As Neelands expands:

Improvisation flexes the muscles of an educator's potential to act on and within the constraints or structure of the imagined situation. It provides the direct lived experience of the tension between social and cultural structures and the capacity for human action. The given circumstances of the improvisation determine the authenticity of what can be said and done.

(Neelands, 2011, p 171)

Positively, improvisation can be learnt and taught (Harris, 2014). However, it will take something of a radical overhaul of accredited lecturer development programmes to build it in – but this is entirely possible, and desirable.

Critical questions for practice

» Do you still give lectures and if so, why? Are there any other better ways of getting across information to people?

» Can you think of ways that you could respect and bring out the knowledge of students in the room on a topic, before you bring in your knowledge, and that of others?

» What are you like at improvising and responding to the room? How would you feel about facing a three-hour session determined by the students? How could you develop your improvising skills?

$\longrightarrow$

» During the Covid-19 pandemic, there was a move to online learning. Are there unexpected benefits that you might want to retain as we return to classroom-based teaching and learning?

» If you are in charge of running a conference or seminar series, or even an individual seminar, how could you do this differently from the traditional abstract submission, Keynote/PowerPoint presentations or seminars with multiple paper format?

Summary

- Traditional approaches to learning and teaching in higher education rarely lend themselves to a critical pedagogic approach.

- We should deconstruct traditional pedagogic approaches, such as the lecture, acknowledge and build on the knowledge in the room, truly embrace being student-led and student-centred and change the ways that we exchange and develop knowledge with each other, by changing the traditional academic conference and seminar.

- Critical pedagogy in teaching and learning is possible, but entails letting go of control and developing improvising skills.

Useful texts

Harris, P (2014) The Youth Worker as Jazz Improviser: Foregrounding Education 'in the Moment' within the Professional Development of Youth Workers. *Professional Development in Education*, 40(4): 654–68.

This article argues for the foregrounding of improvisation and education 'in the moment' within youth workers' professional development, but is transferable to critical pedagogy generally. Through analysis of students' reflective writing, lecturer feedback, interviews with lecturers and video footage of students leading improvised dialogues with their peers, the study sheds light on the challenges and possibilities involved in the teaching and assessment of improvisation in youth work and suggests that students can be encouraged to actively structure their awareness of improvisation and take responsibility for developing a disposition towards it. The author argues that this is important, not only because such improvised practice 'works' instrumentally in terms of engaging young people, many of whom are disengaged from formal education, but because it is also closely aligned ideologically with the value-driven purpose of youth work.

McLoughlin, T, Randolf, L and Seal, M (2021) University as Community: Breaking the Circle of Certainty. In Seal, M (ed) *Hopeful Pedagogies in Higher Education* (pp 208–19). London: Bloomsbury.

In this chapter, Tina, Mike and Lea explore how John Henry Newman's vision of a university was of a community of thinkers, with all staff and students coming together for a common cause. In keeping with a Freirean approach, they encouraged all parties to think differently, be open to mutual learning and committed to working collectively across traditional boundaries. Building on the Freire concept of generative themes, the themes worked through were developed over the course of the week, rather than being decided beforehand. People had to be prepared to take responsibility for firstly bringing ideas, secondly for going through a democratic process to share those ideas and come up with common themes and thirdly taking collective responsibility for developing a vision for these themes to become realities.

Muskett, T A (2017) Popular Education in Practice: A Case Study of Radical Educational Praxis in a Contemporary UK University. In Seal, M (ed) *Trade Union Education: Transforming the World* (pp 216–27). Oxford: New Internationalist.

This chapter is an account of a community of learners (students and staff) who worked together on an elective module, Critical Psychology in Practice, offered to students on an undergraduate psychology degree in the UK. The module was explicitly designed and delivered using democratic and community-based teaching and learning methods, including critical pedagogy. This chapter is about the module. As the authors say, in many ways, it did little that was innovative as it was directly inspired by authentically radical work already undertaken in different cultural contexts. What is more unusual is its setting within a modern UK university as part of a 'mainstream' undergraduate degree programme. They describe how critical pedagogy informed the process of teaching and learning on this course. Finally, they explore some of the complexities associated with its implementation.

Seal, M and Parkes, S (2019) Pedagogy as Transition: Student Directed Tutor Groups on Foundation Years. *Journal of the Foundation Year Network*, 2: 7–20.

This article explores the use of student-led tutor groups, viewed as central to the delivery of the foundation year in social sciences at Newman University. Aimed at 'non-traditional' undergraduate students, the programme in design resists the dominant deficit discourse of undergraduate transition. This means that we do not assume that students have failed in the education system, but that the formal educational and/or societal structures and systems within their experience up until the point of university study have failed them. Central to the approach is a three-hour student-led tutor group that is responsive to student need, rather than requiring delivery of predetermined, set content. The article goes on to explore the underpinning theoretical frames of these tutor groups, tutor roles, skills and experiences and student perspectives.

Chapter 5

Critical pedagogy and the spaces in between

Introduction

Authors such as McLaren (1999) emphasise the importance of creating new spaces for critical pedagogy. John Holloway, in his 2010 book *Crack Capitalism*, argues that it is possible to create cracks, fractures and fissures that forge spaces of rebellion and disrupt the current economic order. A recent book that Mike edited and Alan contributed to, *Hopeful Pedagogies in Higher Education: Dancing in the Cracks*, celebrates and illuminates examples where we can operate in such cracks, and create spaces, in higher education. In that volume, Stephen Cowden, the author of *Acts of Knowing, Critical Pedagogy in, Against and Beyond the University* – another volume that explores the possibilities of critical pedagogy within universities and argues for engagement beyond it – makes the following comment.

The ideas of Critical Pedagogy need to be taken into student groupings, lecturer unions and political organisations where they can provide a framework for an alternative vision of the university. We need to open spaces of resistance outside traditional classrooms – spaces of strikes, spaces of independent student organisation around material questions such as housing, problems with debt, mental health issues, and using 'teach-outs' and other ways of taking critical education into the public space.

(Cowden in Seal (ed), 2021, p 43)

This chapter will explore such spaces in university beyond the classroom where critical pedagogy can be enacted and encouraged. This will include firstly how the Covid crisis has entailed a rethink of what constitutes the classroom, and in turn question what are the relative roles of students and tutor and power in the pedagogic process. We will also consider how we can engage students in both challenging and engaging with the institution, developing critical pedagogic spaces in the partnerships we develop, and finally engaging the wider community in developing critical pedagogic spaces and social actions.

Example 5.1

Practice placements under Covid-19

Relevant principles: *knowledge should be co-created between all participants in the learning process.*

Relevant aims: *to develop critical thinkers who create new knowledge.*

Relevant approaches: *emphasising the importance of democracy and equality in learning environments.*

Because a small number of Alan's youth and community work students needed to complete their placement hours to progress or graduate, and the professional statutory regulatory body (PSRB) had advised courses that online/digital youth work could be counted, he met with the students involved and asked if they would like to be creative. What emerged was a student-led, Facebook welcome group – second-and third-year students created online content, frequently asked questions, chat rooms and even ice-breaker activities for incoming students. Students were asked to think about how it felt when they first came to university, what helped, what worked and what was particularly scary.

Knowing new starters won't really get an immersive experience of induction, and may feel anxious and isolated, they divided the roles and created an online experience that staff could promote through emails to the new cohort. In this way, they have tried to use the virtual world to create a learning community/community of practice, but more significantly, they have removed the formality of a staff-led induction, and used their own lived experience to shape, share and deliver an experience that will be meaningful from a student perspective, and demonstrates what can be achieved through critical pedagogy in practice.

Critiquing the institution

While it may be an area where we are in danger of being accused of boundary blurring, we can support students in asserting their rights. Alan remembers as a first-year student, working with lecturers as allies, challenging the institution on aspects of the course.

Example 5.2

The residential

Relevant principles: *education is inherently political.*

Relevant aims: *to develop critical thinkers who create new knowledge. For people to become aware of their, and others', oppressions.*

Relevant approaches: *emphasising the importance of democracy and equality in learning environments. The importance of cultivating hope and symbolic resistance.*

When Alan was an undergraduate student, the course required students to plan a residential – the task required them working in groups to manage the budget, organise the venue, travel arrangements, programme, etc. Within the group were a small number of parents, who needed childcare support to attend, so a budget was set aside to pay for creche workers. As part of the process, everything had to be presented to the course tutors – they seemed really pleased and said they would get back to the group once the budget was approved by senior management (this seemed reasonable, at the time).

Later that day, the student group were notified that they needed to attend a meeting with tutors; apparently as the HEI Alan was attending did not have an on-site creche or nursery, the 'senior management' had removed the allocated money from the budget! Course tutors were very apologetic, but said we needed to resolve the issue and if we needed to ask them anything, they would be available. At the time, it felt like a very real challenge, but looking back Alan can see how experiential learning was being used to consider inequality, social justice, management and even group work process.

As a class group, people became very impassioned – some wanting to go on the residential, regardless; some who would only go if everyone was able to attend; some fearful that by not attending they would fail the course. Even now, as Alan describes it, he can recall the anger and emotion it generated. It was eventually decided that the group would meet with the course tutors, to say they didn't need a budget, and would run the creche themselves – it felt like a reasonable compromise. The tutors, through conversation, asked if everyone was happy and could see a small level of dissatisfaction and even resentment, when one of them (in what appeared to be a throw-away comment) said, *'you could always refuse to go'* – perhaps Alan's first experience of a teachable moment!

→

It was like permission had been given to be radical to challenge the power holders. Members of the group were tasked with arranging a sit-in, others spoke to other student groups and the Student Union to garner support, a third group spoke to the media – this was serious: the group were convinced that the reputational damage of failing a whole cohort was enough to protect them, and so they went into battle. Over several days, they gained support, the residential was cancelled, they appeared in the local newspaper, the senior management agreed to review the needs of mature students/parents (an on-site creche was opened the following year) and the student group gained immense confidence and a sense of identity.

Alan still doesn't know if the whole experience was stage-managed, but he does remember that sense of achievement and self-confidence that it gave the group, although even after this example of student protest and challenge to the power-holders, the group happily completed a reflective essay on their learning, as there needed to be an assessment task. From critical pedagogy in practice to conformity and a return to the normal order of things.

More recently, there has been a desire within some universities to address the white, Eurocentric, hetero-normative curriculum, whether that has been through module content or bibliographies. Alongside this, the National Union of Students have been organising a campaign to decolonise the curriculum, and many universities are now consciously addressing this. At Leeds Beckett University, students have been recruited as Black, Asian and Minoritised Ethnicity/Black, Asian and Minority Ethnic (BAME) Ambassadors: they work with staff and attend power-holding committees and meetings with the most senior staff of the university.

Alan is currently working with some of the BAME Ambassadors and Student Union Sabbatical Officers to help support the Centre for Learning and Teaching, the central service which provides staff development activities (among other things), planning staff–student facilitation of workshops around issues of inclusivity and race, in the first instance. Mike has similarly been engaged at Suffolk in the setting up of a decolonising the curriculum group, which has evolved into an anti-racist alliance, which involves all staff and students examining and challenging racism within the institution – presently it has a focus on examining placements and the negative experiences of students.

Example 5.3

Christmas trees and movie nights

Relevant principles: *education is inherently political.*

Relevant aims: *for people to make connections between personal experiences and wider societal forces.*

Relevant approaches*: the importance of cultivating hope and symbolic resistance.*

At Newman University, the critical pedagogy group and the Romero Freire Institute are uniquely made up of representatives from academics, professional and support staff, students, alumni and members of the local community. The institute has broad reach and acts as a bridge and mediator between student and community research, consultancy and evaluation, the scholarship of teaching and learning and academic research in higher education.

The institute is not just about seminar series and the writing of books. They are committed to engaging in institutional issues and the development of generative themes that lead to action. A campaign was launched around the Christmas tree. Every year a corporate tree was erected, decorated by an outside company. We challenged this and proposed that the tree should instead be sourced from a community group, and preferably decorated by them. Estates and Finance resisted this change, feeling that the tree might not be decorated to a sufficient 'quality' if left to community groups.

We set up a stall involving community members to create decorations in the Christmas week and then presented them to senior management to show they were of sufficient quality. We were allowed to decorate the tree. On another occasion we supported a student who was encountering institutional barriers to putting on a local community movie night by providing a home for the night, a pedagogic justification for the endeavour and agreeing to staff the event (the old chestnut of not being insured was being invoked).

Critical issues

The danger of tokenism and hidden power

However, initiatives such as those mentioned in this chapter cannot exist without a genuine attempt to reimagine the role of students, no longer the passive receivers of learning, or the tokenistic representative at course committees – we must embrace active participation in all levels of higher education, not just discussions about the curriculum or teaching and learning activities. Students need to be similarly engaged with Governance and Quality.

While we give examples of how research and community engagement can be enabled through critical pedagogic approaches, this takes commitment from the institution and an understanding of the approach. If the research gets the wrong kind of funding or the wrong kind of outputs in terms of the Research Excellence Framework (REF), it can very quickly be sidelined. Community development and engagement can similarly be funnelled and constructed through other institutional concerns, such as the need for Impact Case Studies. Community groups Mike has worked with have talked about a 'cycle of REF abuse', whereby two years before the REF universities suddenly want to work with them and forge partnerships, only to disappear again for five years until the next REF cycle.

Power within critical pedagogy groups

Power can still operate within groups dedicated to critical pedagogy. Critiques of Freire say that rather than ameliorating power differentials, he merely hides them, as Taylor expands.

The rhetoric which announced the importance of dialogue, engagement, and equality, and denounced silence, massification and oppression, did not match in practice the subliminal messages and modes of a Banking System of education. Albeit benign, Freire's approach differs only in degree, but not in kind, from the system which he so eloquently criticizes.

(1993, p 148)

To give an example, a permanent source of debate and tension in the Romero Freire Institute was the divide between academic and support and professional staff. This existed at a cultural level that was then reinscribed at a structural level. Members of professional and support staff had to attend meetings in their lunch times, as their line managers did not deem it relevant to their job. We approached the vice chancellor who agree to send an email to all line managers saying that attendance of this group was relevant to all staff, and they should be released time to attend. Members of the group also had to challenge themselves. Once, academic members could not attend a meeting because they were on an academic staff away day so they changed the meeting venue to the away day venue and held it at lunchtime; other staff rightly pointed out that this not only excluded them, but also it revealed the assumptions of power to do this within the academic group members – the operation of this was thoroughly worked through.

Engaging with Professional, Statutory and Regulatory Bodies

Engaging with PSRBs might feel like an infrequent activity only related to validations and approvals. However, most of these bodies are obliged, and want, to engage with practitioners in the development of their frameworks and standards. While consultations can often feel tokenistic, we should reflect on how easy it is to blame the regulators and project onto them, as we sometimes do with the quality processes that our institutions have – a phenomenon already covered. Indeed, a friend of ours within quality has said that they sometimes rail against and blame PSRBs as a way of deflecting the antagonism they get from academics.

Example 5.4

Working with the National Youth Agency

Relevant principles: *knowledge should relate to the lived experience of participants. Knowledge should be co-created between all participants in the learning process.*

Relevant aims: *to develop critical thinkers who create new knowledge.*

Relevant approaches: *emphasising the importance of democracy and equality in learning environments.*

Through Alan's work with the National Youth Agency, Education and Training Standards Committee (England) – the Professional, Statutory and Regulatory Body for Youth and Community Work qualifications, he has previously helped shape the curriculum for professional education, acting

$\longrightarrow$

as a critical friend when the Quality Assurance Agency was developing Subject Benchmarks, and helping refine and develop the validation approval processes. But his most significant achievement was supporting the first-ever student elected to the committee, and eventually seeing her take on the role as a member of a validation panel for a university developing new youth and community work provision. Since then, he has worked with other students and members of the committee to ensure student representation is embedded in the work of the committee, and where possible students can engage in validation activities.

Critical pedagogy within wider partnerships

Most institutions cite partnership within their mission statements and aims as being central. Mike and Alan have found it possible to build in critical pedagogy as an essential feature of partnerships, be that about research, teaching or knowledge exchange.

Example 5.5

Work with the General Federation of Trade Unions

Relevant principles: *education is inherently political.*

Relevant aims: *to develop critical thinkers who create new knowledge.*

Relevant approaches: *the importance of cultivating hope and symbolic resistance.*

Both Alan and Mike were approached by the General Federation of Trade Unions (GFTU) several years ago to lead their political education committee in developing a strategic approach to trade union education and to bring in educational ideas from critical pedagogy and popular education. The strategic approach had three strands: developing a body of knowledge, developing continuing professional development (CPD) opportunities and developing standards. We initiated and edited a book on trade union education utilising worldwide authors commissioned by *New Internationalist*. An external colleague comments:

The committee was responsible for leading the development of the post-graduate training, as well as co-ordinating and editing the first Trade Union

Education book in many years, already a best-seller and recognised by Trade Union leadership as ground-breaking.

It was cited at the recent Momentum conference as 'the book to read' on trade union education. Importantly, authors included activists as well as academics. We set up a support programme for activist writers, who were often suffering from imposter syndrome about their writing. *New Internationalist* subsequently set up an imprint with the GFTU for trade union books centring on radical education. We are on the editorial board and have initiated and commented on a number of new publications from new and established authors. We also undertook the presentation of the committee's works at the GFTU's last two union building conferences.

Building on these developments we developed a graduate certificate (level 4) which has been run by Leeds Beckett University aimed at activist educators, and a post-graduate certificate in critical trade union education aimed at their tutors run at Newman. Both have run successfully. One union has incorporated the courses into their CPD framework, describing the courses as '*having the biggest impact on their political education and general approach to education that we can remember*' (Union education manager). In total, over 50 learners have undertaken the course with 50 per cent not having previous teaching qualifications, and others having little formal education. Several participants have gone on to develop educational programmes within their unions and on to further study. They are now a mainstay of the GFTU training programme.

Critical pedagogy and wider community engagement

Community involvement and development is similarly and invariably a key feature of most higher education institutions' key aims and missions. What they often seem to be unsure about is how to go about it, and this is where critical pedagogues can be useful and central to the institution. Mike was the strategic lead on community development in the institution. Previously the institution accepted that their strategy had not worked. Mike worked with senior management including the vice chancellor, making the strategic links and building the relationships with local stakeholders.

Example 5.6

Involvement with Citizens UK

Relevant principles: *education is inherently political.*

Relevant aims: *for people to make connections between personal experiences and wider societal forces.*

Relevant approaches: *the importance of cultivating hope and symbolic resistance.*

Mike was instrumental in Newman becoming a founder member of Citizens UK Birmingham, an independent and non-partisan civil society alliance of faith, education, trade union and community groups, acting together for the common good of the city. Students and support staff were participants, leaders and co-researchers.

Staff, academic, professional and support and administrative from across all schools, have engaged very much on a mutual and egalitarian basis in strategic initiatives. Students lead an action group with a number of community groups. This included successfully lobbying three Clinical Commissioning Groups about mental health provision for 16–17 year-olds resulting in change in their entire strategy for young people, and involving Newman staff and students in its redesign. Other evidence includes: winning 'campaign of the year' in 2014 and 'action of the year' in 2015; actively leading and achieving large turnouts on two major campaigns; leading on Newman becoming a living wage employer, sitting on the West Midlands refugee welcome board, sponsoring refugee students and families and successfully encouraging other universities to follow suit. Students have seen the benefits of wider community involvement:

The best part of the course was where they got us to be involved in some of the real life actions of Citizens UK, it made the subject come alive and feel real.

Sometimes courses feel a bit vague and abstract, but not this bit, it reminded me of why I wanted to work with young people.

Citizens UK Birmingham features in the *Birmingham Post*'s Power 250 list for the region and is credited by public agency leaders for being 'ahead of the curve' on working for the common good. The organisation states: '*This has been possible because of the commitment shown by founding members like Newman University*'.

In their words:

A number of our community leaders who run very successful third sector organisations in the city are alumni from Newman. Newman students and former students are present on every single action team within Citizens.

Other tangible successes include establishing local shops and community buildings as safe havens near schools, securing the backing of elected and business leaders to pay the living wage and Birmingham committing to resettle 500 Syrian refugees from UN camps. Softer impacts have included the local community feeling that the university is serious in its commitment to them and students and staff feeling more confident, empowered and knowledgeable of the local community's issues.

Newman University has also set up an accredited community leadership course with citizens. There is a recognised need from the government (DCLG, 2010) for the development of effective community leaders. Within this, the government recognises the worth of community organising, the specific approach of this course. It features high in their localism agenda. They have funded the training of up to 5000 community organisers through the NGO Locality, although this is not formally accredited. There was not, to date, an accredited course aimed at community leaders, the target group for the community leadership certificate. To date, over 150 students have passed the course. Evaluations have shown that the course has increased community leaders' confidence, skills and leaders and employability with significant numbers of students who have no previous degree-level qualifications going on to degree-level study, citing the course as the catalyst of this.

Example 5.7

Critical pedagogy, community and research

Relevant principles: *knowledge should relate to the lived experience of participants.*

Relevant aims: *for people to become aware of their, and others', oppressions. For people to make connections between personal experiences and wider societal forces.*

Relevant approaches: *the importance of cultivating hope and symbolic resistance.*

→

> Students in a research campaign, funded by Newman University, gathered testimonials from Muslims and non-Muslims for a commission on Islam and Public Life chaired by Dominic Grieve QC MP and 20 others. A student delegation was looking at the role of the university. This had a real impact, as the commission organiser commented:
>
> *I just wanted to send a note to say thank you for your testimony and contribution to the Citizens UK Commission on Islam, Participation and Public Life in Birmingham. The Commissioners are really grateful for your time and your insights. The discussion was incredibly rich and will be instrumental in shaping our final recommendations.*

Conclusion

As a child, Mike used to think that teachers got into a box at the end of the lesson, to emerge from it the next day to teach him – he could not imagine his teachers as people with concerns outside of school, and even if they did, he could not imagine that they might find common cause together. It is vital to find spaces in between to break down such perceptions and the atomising dehumanising tendencies of the neoliberal modern capitalist university. As Stephen Cowden, quoted in the opening to this chapter, states:

These different spaces of engagement allow issues people face to be addressed not managerially as concerns of 'consumer satisfaction' but as the political issues they are, with a real presence in everyday life. These are all potentially spaces where students can break out of the pervasiveness of the discourse of marketisation where they are the consumers of learning to a place where they can begin to see the potential of their own agency as creators of knowledge.

(Cowden, 2021, p 43)

The examples given in this chapter are just a starting point. Other examples could include working with Student Unions to develop a meaningful 'student voice' that ensures their full contribution to the life of a university from module and course level. We also need to change how we see our alumni, moving away from seeing them as a source of revenue, or of good luck stories, which are again about raising revenue. They are our partners and colleagues with whom we can change their, and our, university together, including how we produce and reproduce knowledge, and allow higher education's true potential to flourish. As Mike Neary and Joss Winn describe in their chapter 'Student as Producer'.

This requires academics and students to do more than simply redesign their curricula, but go further and redesign the organizing principle (i.e. private property and wage labour), through which academic knowledge is currently being produced. An exemplar alternative organizing principle is already proliferating in universities in the form of open, networked collaborative initiatives which are not intrinsically anti-capital but, fundamentally, ensure the free and creative use of research materials.

(Neary and Winn, 2009, p 2080)

Critical questions for practice

» How have you taken the opportunities of the Covid crisis to expose, deconstruct and reconstruct your power in the classroom? How would you feel about doing this?

» How could you meaningfully involve your students in challenging aspects of the institution that negatively impact on them?

» What opportunities for positive engagement – where you could have a meaningful partnership with students outside the classroom – are offered by the university structures?

» How would you incorporate some of the principles of critical pedagogy in the partnerships you develop, the community groups you engage and the research that you bid for?

Summary

• Critical pedagogy in spaces in between is crucial to expand and define our relationships outside of the classroom and become a true partner in learning.

• It is possible to engage in meaningful spaces that define the learning spaces, critique and engage the institution and professional bodies.

• Critical pedagogy can also reshape the partnerships we develop, the research we undertake and the communities we engage.

Useful texts

Cowden, S and Singh, G (2013) *Acts of Knowing: Critical Pedagogy In, Against and Beyond the University*. London: Bloomsbury Publishing.

Acts of Knowing aims to provide readers with a means of understanding the issues from the perspective of critical pedagogy; this is an educational philosophy which believes that 'knowing' must be freed from the constraints of the financial and managerialist logics which dominate the contemporary university. Critical pedagogy is important for three key reasons: firstly it conceptualises pedagogy as a process of engagement between the teacher and taught; secondly that that engagement is based on an underlying humanistic view about human worth and value; and thirdly that the 'knowing' which can come out of this engagement needs to be understood essentially as exchange between people, rather than a financial exchange. Cowden and Singh argue that the conception of education as simply a means for securing economic returns for the individual and for the society's positioning in a global marketplace represents a fundamentally impoverished conception of education, which impoverishes not just individuals, but society as a whole.

Neary, M and Winn, J (2009) The Student as Producer: Reinventing the Student Experience in Higher Education. In Bell, L, Neary, M and Stevenson, H (eds) *The Future of Higher Education: Policy, Pedagogy and the Student Experience* (pp 192–210). London: Bloomsbury Publishing.

In this chapter, Neary and Winn set out to provide an overview of recent critical responses to the corporatisation of higher education and the configuration of the student as consumer. They also discuss the relationship between the core activities of teaching and research and reflect on both nineteenth-century discourse and more recent efforts to re-establish the university as a liberal humanist institution, where teaching and research are equal and fundamental aspects of academic life. While recognising recent efforts which acknowledge and go some way to addressing the need for enquiry-based learning and constructivist models of student participation, the authors argue that a more critical approach is necessary to promote change at an institutional level. This critical approach looks at the wider social, political and economic context beyond the institution and introduces the work of Benjamin and other Marxist writers who have argued that a critique of the social relations of capitalist production is central to understanding and remodeling the role of the university and the relationship between academic and student.

Seal, M (ed) (2021) *Hopeful Pedagogies in Higher Education: Dancing in the Cracks.* London and New York: Bloomsbury Press.

While acknowledging the problems associated with trying to enact critical pedagogy in higher education, this book attempts to rescue critical pedagogy, locating some of its associated pessimism as a misreading of Freire and offering hopeful avenues for new theory and practice. These misreadings are also located in the present, in the assumption that unless change comes within the lifetime of the project, it has somehow failed. Instead, this book argues that a positive utopianism is possible. Present actions need to be celebrated, and cultivated as symbols of hope, possibility and generativity for the future – which the concept of hope implies. The contributors make the case for celebrating the pedagogies of HE that operate in liminal spaces – situated in the spaces between the present and the future (between the world as it is and the world as it could be) and also in the cracks that are beginning to show in the dominant discourses.

| **Critical pedagogy in higher education institutions**

Critical pedagogy is fundamentally democratic, informal, non-hierarchical with a curriculum determined by participants that privileges the oppressed and their perspectives, and is committed to action. Higher education, conversely, is often un-democratic, formal, hierarchical, with a curriculum determined by tutors or national bodies, and often re-inscribes existing privileges and is distant from lived experience.

(Seal, 2020, p 134)

Introduction

As Mike expressed above, in some ways higher education seems the least likely place for critical pedagogy to take place. Many contemporary accounts express a deep cynicism about being able to enact and enable critical pedagogy with integrity in higher education (Cowden and Singh, 2013; Van Heertum, 2006). Nevertheless, in the conclusion to that same book Mike notes that unlike in schools, in higher education, staff develop the curriculum, devise the teaching, learning and assessment strategy, quality assure and assess courses. This is also done relatively close to the ground, at lecturing team and programme manager level. We therefore have a lot of potential to enact critical pedagogy within higher education in a way that other education sectors do not. In this chapter we will examine the necessary conditions in higher education for critical pedagogy to flourish. We argue that critical pedagogues need to work both on the ground, developing our pedagogic practice, at a strategic level, engaging with such questions as what a university is for, and, crucially, within a collective – it is very hard to operate as a lone critical pedagogue, and to try to do so is against the spirit of critical pedagogy.

Example 6.1

Critical pedagogy collectives

At Newman University, the critical pedagogy group and the Romero Freire Institute are uniquely made up of representatives from academics, professional and support staff, students, alumni and members of the local community. The institute has broad reach and acts as a bridge and mediator between student and community research, consultancy and evaluation, the scholarship of teaching and learning and academic research in higher education.

While it has taken two years, the critical pedagogy group now has active participation of students. It has also greatly influenced embedding critical pedagogy into the curriculum and is about to produce a book based on its endeavours. The institute has had a successful seminar series, involving students, academics and professional staff.

Through Alan's work with the Centre for Learning and Teaching at Leeds Beckett University, he has co-developed a Critical Pedagogy Practitioners Network, which helped shape the inputs for a university-wide conference.

Critical issues

What is higher education for? The importance of strategic engagement

It is vital to question what higher education is for. An answer is the basis of many of the mission statements and strategic plans of universities. To engage with the question, and to consequently engage with the formation of these plans and statements, gives critical pedagogues much leverage. Debates about the purpose of a university have been conducted for centuries. Mahon (2014) usefully breaks down the functions of a university into knowledge and cultural production, civic responsibility and economic development. Giroux (2010) and Walker (2002) see the university as being about the formation of citizens who can participate meaningfully in public and the formation of a society characterised by a healthy, *'inclusive democracy'* (Giroux, 2010, p 190). Mahon (2014) sees the university's role as offering a social critique as part of its civic duty (Bleiklie, 1998; Giroux, 2010; Shore and Wright, 2004) in that we should engage in public political debate. Economically, we are involved in the formation of professionals (Lee and Dunston, 2011) and providing products and research that economically benefit society. These functions are detectable in the current emphasis on impact within research, although many (eg, Mahon, 2014) would see this as a constraining factor and in tension with the first two themes of knowledge and cultural production.

Bleiklie (1998) says most universities have developed a specific economic focus that reinscribes capitalist and neoliberalist thought, ie what is good for the market is good for society, and that we are *'educating people for*

⟶

the new economy' (Altbach et al, 2009, p 5). However, words like 'civic duty', 'the wider community' and 'common good' are often foregrounded in university mission statements and can act as leverage. However, in the strategic plans that roll out these missions, we often see that community is interpreted as the business community and the common good framed in economic terms of GDP, ignoring income differentials. Nevertheless, such declarations give us leverage to hold our institutions to account for realising their mission statements and offering different articulations of these missions in the strategic plans that go beyond the economic, and expose and re-own terms like civic responsibility and the common good when they are used reductively.

However, the strategic challenge is difficult to do in isolation. It is often best coming from a collective, a learning community, and one with critical pedagogy as its focus. In Mike's previous institution the critical pedagogy group very much influenced the development of the strategic plan. The leadership involved the group in the planning process and adopted some of the principles of critical pedagogy in running consultation sessions. They were asked to write the introductory section of the strategic plan, examining our 'human approach to pedagogy' and articulating our pedagogic values for both the learning and teaching strategy and the institution's new strategic plan. They then used the plan to justify research, pedagogic approaches and the setting up of a research and teaching institute within the university.

Being a critical pedagogue in the university

While we have given examples of how a lecturer can enable and enact critical pedagogy in higher education, it seems useful to step back and consider some general principles for it to thrive. Motta (2013, p 123) gives some interesting pointers for pedagogic practice within and outside of the classroom. Firstly, she calls for a new, or renewed, type of relationship to be had with students. This means engaging with our students' lives and, when needed, representing and advocating their complexities and subjectivities. This can be particularly important within higher education where the systems are designed for a particular kind of student who does not have such a complicated life (Parkes et al, 2018).

This may also mean sharing our own subjectivities, and vulnerabilities, to expose the projected norm as being a discriminatory construction. Motta calls for '*epistemological disobedience*' (Mignolo, 2009) in that we should disrupt norms of emotional and bodily practices of the university (Motta, 2013, p 107). This means lecturers as well as students are encouraged to be open about their biographies, including not only discussion of professional challenges within their own practice, but also personal reflections on experiences as members of privileged hegemonic and marginalised and oppressed groups – often concurrently.

Motta (2013) then asks us to create participatory and democratic experiences. And while this is something to be worked towards, they need to be actively created with the students from the outset. This is not always an easy process. As noted in the previous chapter, students and lecturers may resist democratisation. It is not what people are used to and carries responsibility. To embrace it may need pedagogic intervention. Also, higher education structures will limit this democracy, although not as much as we think, as we explored in the chapter on pedagogy.

Motta (2013) also talks about 'working with power and empathy', challenging who is the learner and the learned, the nature of pedagogical relationships and who has the right to create knowledge. That the creation of knowledge is a process of co-creation needs to be emphasised from the beginning of the programme and integrated throughout. Lecturers should not privilege their own intelligence and insights, recognising them to be inherently partial and contingent, and this needs to be named, continually.

Example 6.2

Deconstructing the presentation

Mike attended a conference in Bangladesh, as an ordinary attendee and was quickly asked to speak about critical pedagogy as a presentation. In his presentation he asked why he had been invited to open the conference – a white western male, with a title of professor – was their indigenous knowledge (Smith, 1999), not a better starting point? He also publicly asked himself why he had colluded with being invited to speak.

Embracing empathy means that critical pedagogy is an intersubjective experience (Benjamin, 1998). Existential notions of encounter and intersubjective notions of recognition (Benjamin, 2017; Butler, 1990) combined with elements of hooks' (1994) engaged pedagogue seem relevant. We need to explicitly work through the visceral, embodied experience of educational spaces and bring tacit, sometimes unconscious, processes into a learnable, theoretical framework (Harris et al, 2017). We also need to recognise the performativity of this and actively challenge the prescribed roles of student and lecturer (Baizerman, 1989; Butler, 1990).

Motta (2013) also calls for working in areas of discomfort. This includes the tears, anger, guilt and fear that goes with real exchanges and ultimately makes for 'real' bonds. This entails dealing with raw, often previously hidden, emotions and projections; any of the negative expressions of this need to be absorbed, detoxified and rearticulated. Such difficult processes are central and a part of students re-examining their social positioning and oppression. It allows for seemingly trivial and significant aspects of their own lives to be first discovered, named, and then imbued with meaning. These processes of oppression are not just operational between students and lecturers. It also manifests between support and professional staff, and academic staff. This was played out continually in the critical pedagogy group as we explored earlier, but the critical pedagogy group continues to keep working the dynamics through.

The importance of working with others

While being the lone maverick critical pedagogue within an institution may have some romantic attraction, most evidence suggests this is very difficult, and perhaps not desirable to try (Kumashiro, 2002; Seal, 2019). Unless you are particularly high up in the structure, it is also questionable what strategic influence you can have. One is in danger of becoming the tolerated dissenter espousing radical views and used as evidence of the supposed plurality of academic voices in the institution, but in reality you are marginalised and marginal.

A common theme in the literature is the key role a strong learning community plays in fostering praxis (Mahon, 2014; Seal, 2020). Features of such a learning community include a commitment to co-operation (Braa and Callero, 2006, p 360), a spirit of trust and respectfulness (Gibbs et al, 2004; Hardy, 2010), concern for the creation of 'safe' spaces (Breunig, 2005; Hardy, 2010), a culture of mentoring (Gibbs et al, 2004), a social justice commitment (Gibbs et al, 2004) and scholarly dialogue and activity that promotes collaborative and individual self-inquiry into pedagogy (Hardy, 2010; Jacobs, 2008).

However, a group cannot just exist in isolation, else it becomes just a different silo or place of retreat. We need to look at what internal conditions are needed for a critical pedagogy community of practice to flourish. Mahon (2014) uses the frame of 'practice architecture', exploring how practices prefigure, and are prefigured by, the sites in which they are located and how professional practices are enabled and constrained by those sites. She names a number of levels at which practice architectures operate – *cultural-discursive* (such as university mission; discourses regarding pedagogy), *material-economic* (such as allocation of staff to subjects; employment of casual versus continuing staff; workshop spaces; staff meeting spaces; workload allocation; staff–student ratios; study leave) and *social-political* (such as decision-making; surveillance measures; power attached to particular positions) dimensions of the social world (Kemmis and Grootenboer, 2008).

Mahon found collegial relationships and opportunities for collaboration within the academic community to be essential as *'sources of solidarity, inspiration, information, and as sites of critical exchanges and stirring each other into critical language'* (Mahon, 2014, p 164). Other enablers include student engagement, student feedback, positive student–teacher relationships, opportunities for dialogue and research and engagement with issues within and beyond the institution (Mahon, 2014 p 76). Mahon (2014) also catalogues disablers including the intensification of academic work, the lack of (or diminishing) teacher–student contact time, challenges of online teaching, over-regulation and standardisation of practice, promotion of technical, virtual, neo-liberal constructions of pedagogical practice and a shift from a critical and collegial culture to one of compliance and competition.

Disablers are certainly points of discussion within the critical pedagogy group. We help each other and highlight that people are not alone, and different models of practice are invoked and articulated. At an institutional level, Mike has have sought to influence the culture of teaching and learning and staff pedagogic development at Newman through the group and through the Learning and Teaching Committee, and now the learning and teaching strategy. At our instigation critical pedagogy was a strand within 2018's teaching and learning conference and was the basis of the approach in 2019 and 2020 and will be for subsequent ones (it informed the 2021 conference at Leeds Beckett University). A collaborative organising team of students, professional and support staff and academics was established, and we explored how we work together to support student success. Mike's then Director of Learning, Teaching and Scholarship, himself a National Teaching Fellow, said of the conference:

The conference was a powerful example of hopeful, collaborative partnership working and proved generative of positive proposals to enhance the student learning experience across the university. It would not have been possible without the critical pedagogy group's expert facilitation, example and leadership.

To give another example, a day was given over to looking at the National Student Survey (NSS) and pedagogic practice in Mike's school. Mike was invited to participate and shape the day. It moved from showcasing those who had successful pedagogies (ie they had high NSS scores) to showcasing all, recognising that NSS scores do not necessarily reflect quality. Similarly, a wish to explore why we had scored badly on our fairness criteria moved from deriding the Teaching Excellent Framework (TEF) and how we can 'game' the scores to a plan to explore with students what 'fairness' means in HE, and how to work on this together and have meaningful dialogue.

Critical pedagogy and research

While a critical pedagogy group or collective is one approach, it is not the only way to enact critical pedagogy in the institution. One approach is critical pedagogy and research. Participatory research is written about quite comprehensively (Cooke and Kothari, 2001; Cornwall, 2003; Kesby et al, 2007; Seal, 2018; Servaes et al, 1996) and is often closely linked to critical pedagogy (Seal, 2018). Its theoretical and practical applications are covered particularly in the work of Chambers (2002, 2010; Ghaye et al, 2008) at the Institute of Development Studies, and in terms of co-enquiry in the work of Heron (1996) and community-based research (Fals-Borda and Rahman, 1991; Hills et al, 2000; Israel et al, 1998; Savan and Sider, 2003). Authors such as Chambers (2010), who advocate for participatory research, claim that traditional processes of research are often rarefied and mystified, and that much research is therefore done 'on' people by 'experts', rather than with or for them, re-enforcing people's distancing from and cynicism towards it. Participatory research seeks to be the opposite of this.

One way that this is commonly operationalised is through staff–student partnerships. Many institutions have staff–student partnerships and they are great potential vehicle for taking a critical pedagogic approach – some partnership models are based on critical pedagogic approaches.

Example 6.3

Staff–student partnerships

Staff–student partnerships are a part of enabling a participatory culture with students. At Newman these partnerships have impacted at several levels. At a cultural-discursive level, many participants felt that their project had had a direct influence over an aspect of the curriculum or wider student experience at Newman. At a material-economic level the scheme has been both funded and attracted funding. Finally, at a social-political level, some have said doors within the institution 'aren't open', while others sensed the projects were not yet routinely 'touching institutional structures'. The Romero Freire Institute aims to help in facilitating this dialogue and aims to have reached senior management level, and so be embedded within Newman's structures.

For more on this approach, look at the work of John Peters and Leoarna Mathias. (See useful texts.)

Conclusion

Finally, Mahon (2014) provides a useful set of criteria for an institution to consider in supporting critical pedagogy, which is also useful for anyone considering setting up a community of practice around critical pedagogy.

1   Allow time (eg for reflection, relationship-building, scholarship, noticing, engaging in debate, democratic/inclusive decision-making, creating conditions of possibility).

2   Allow space for creativity.

3   Allow space for autonomy and flexibility so that educators can exercise professional judgement, be responsive and respond appropriately.

4   Foster/sustain/allow the development of positive, productive, trusting relationships.

5   Encourage/legitimise/provide for critical dialogue and reflexive inquiry and conversation.

6   Provide opportunities for maximum engagement in community and opportunities to develop the capacity for critical pedagogical praxis through experience.

We think that with these conditions, the right people and the right will, meaningful critical pedagogy is possible in higher education still.

Critical questions for practice

»   How have you tried to enact critical pedagogy within the university, either as a lone maverick or as part of a collective?

»   How engaged have you been in staff–student partnerships if they exist in your institution, and have you tried to get involved and develop them?

»   Do your practice and your institution meet the criteria for meaningful critical pedagogy to be enacted?

»   Have you tried to involve critical pedagogy practice in your research; how are the subjects of the research involved in designing, planning and carrying out your research?

Summary

- Despite the marketisation of higher education and the ascendancy of neoliberalism and neo-managerialism, meaningful critical pedagogy is still possible within higher education.

- Strategic engagement is needed at the mission and strategic plan level of the institution, re-asking what is the nature of a university, and how do we relate to the communities we are meant to serve.

- Mahon has coined some relevant characteristics of the conditions for critical pedagogy to flourish, and the practice architectures that are needed to enable that flourishing.

- Critical pedagogy is best enacted as a collective within an institution.

Useful texts

Bovill, C (2020) *Co-creating Learning and Teaching: Towards Relational Pedagogy in Higher Education*. St Albans: Critical Publishing.

This book focuses on co-creation of learning and teaching, where students and staff collaborate to design curricula or elements of curricula is an important pedagogical idea within higher education, key to meaningful learner engagement and building positive student–staff relationships. Drawing on literature from schools' education, and using a range of examples from universities worldwide, this book highlights the benefits of classroom-level, relational, dialogic pedagogy and co-creation. It includes a focus on the classroom as the site of co-creation, examples of practice and practical guidance, and a unique perspective in bringing together the concept of co-creation with relational pedagogy within higher education learning and teaching.

Mahon, K (2014) Critical Pedagogical Praxis in Higher Education. PhD thesis, Charles Stuart University. [online] Available at: https://researchoutput.csu.edu.au/en/publications/critical-pedagogical-praxis-in-higher-education-3 (accessed 25 June 2021).

While unpublished, this is one of the few pieces of research to examine the efforts of a group of academics to enact critical pedagogical praxis (individually and collectively) within a university. It catalogues how they were enabled and constrained by the conditions within their setting, and how the academics negotiated tensions between the conditions and their praxis-oriented goals. Elsewhere Mike talks about the tyranny of peer review and how it can constrain and narrow rather than legitimise knowledge (Seal, 2014). The research highlighted that university conditions can be a source of nourishment or tension for critical pedagogical praxis depending on whether they create and/or limit time and space for (a) building positive collegial and student–teacher relationships; (b) engaging in critical, reflexive inquiry, and rigorous critical conversation; (c) responding creatively and ethically to people and situations; and (d) engaging in professional learning and critically reflective pedagogical practice. The research suggested that, in order to reclaim universities as niches for critical pedagogical praxis, there is a need for some university arrangements to be more closely scrutinised and/or reoriented, and for new, more sustaining arrangements to be created. Stories of the lived critical pedagogical praxis of the participating academics provided important insights into how this can be achieved.

Motta, S (2013) Pedagogies of Possibility In, Against and Beyond the Imperial Patriarchal Subjectivities of Higher Education. In Cowden, S and Singh, S (eds) *Acts of Knowing: Critical Pedagogy In, Against and Beyond the University* (pp 85–124). London: Bloomsbury Publishing.

This chapter discusses the authors' experience of introducing critical pedagogy into an MA course in an elite university. She critically interrogates the assumed resonances and compatibilities between critical pedagogy and institutionally recognised (and produced) 'critical' subjectivities. The author conceptualises and analyses the relative openness and closure in student subjectivities to a critical pedagogy committed to multiplicity, horizontalism and 'otherness'. The author develops a pedagogical pragmatics (Gillespie et al, 2002) in light of her reflections and talks about what this has taught her in thinking about what critical pedagogy as political project actually represents. She concludes with a discussion and analysis of student experiences of this teaching.

Peters, J and Mathias, L (2018) Enacting Student Partnership as Though We Really Mean It: Some Freirean Principles for a Pedagogy of Partnership. *International Journal for Students as Partners*, 2(2): 53–70.

This article is driven by a concern that while the idea of student–staff partnership working is becoming increasingly popular in higher education, there is a risk that, as the idea spreads, the radical nature of partnership working can be diluted and domesticated by established power structures. It explores the theoretical and practical implications of adopting approaches to partnership working informed by the ideas of Paulo Freire. The authors see this as a partnership working with a political point – consciously seeking to resist the forces of neoliberalism and any attempts to domesticate partnership to that paradigm. Pedagogy of partnership, informed by Freire, is juxtaposed with neoliberal domesticated partnership, and six principles are offered for enacting partnership as though we really mean it.

Seal, M (2018) *Participatory Pedagogic Impact Research: Co-production with Community Partners in Action.* London: Routledge.

The book makes a case for research to be a synthesis of participatory research, critical pedagogy, peer research and community organising. It develops a model called Participatory Pedagogic Impact Research (PPIR). Participatory research is often criticised for not having the impact it promises. PPIR ensures that the issues chosen, and the recommendations developed, serve the mutual self-interest of stakeholders, are realistic and realisable. At the same time this approach pushes the balance of power towards the oppressed using methods of dissemination that hold decision makers to account and create real change. PPIR also develops a robust method for creatively identifying issues, methods and analytic frameworks. Its third section details case studies across Europe and the United States of PPIR in action with professional researchers' and community partners' reflections on these experiences.

Chapter 7 | Future agendas for critical pedagogy in higher education

Introduction

We hope that this book has gone some way towards making lecturing a less lonely business, and while it may well not have alleviated the stress inherent in neoliberal higher education institutions, it might have provided some tools for understanding our own oppressions. We also hope that it has ignited or rekindled some passion for teaching. Positively you can become a Reader and Professor in learning and teaching now. However, learning and teaching is still seen very much as secondary to research, even in teaching-intensive universities, and in reality, budding Readers and Professors in learning and teaching are still judged on their research and writing about learning and teaching, rather than the actual practice of pedagogy itself. Learning and teaching can all too often be viewed by those 'traditional academics' as a route people take if their subject research is not up to scratch. The impact of this on academics who want to teach is either a resentment about those around them who gain recognition and promotion, or a sense of 'imposter syndrome' where they feel like a second-class academic.

Perversely, this is an old university model of what makes for an academic – or more precisely a new university's fantasy about what they think an academic should be, based on a myth about old universities which stopped being accurate, if it ever was, decades ago. It is also an unrealistic model if you work in new universities, which Mike and Alan do – the potential to undertake research is shrinking. Research council funding, and increasingly any source of funding, is concentrated in Russell Group universities and in STEM subjects (MillionPlus, 2016). However, what we can research, and be a scholar of, is our students and our learning and teaching experiences, and ultimately our impact can change people's lives through the work of our students.

We hope we have shown that there is room to shake up our education experience and do things differently. However, we need to start with ourselves. Given the sustained critique of lectures as a medium (Clark, 2018), we have to ask ourselves, why are they still used? It goes deeper than moving away from a tired pedagogic approach. Mike remembers giving a lecture at a foundation year conference on pedagogy. Foundation year lecturers are often the lowest-status academics (they don't even teach at higher education level!). They are often on short-term, part-time teaching-only contracts. Mike asked those assembled '*Why do we still give lectures?*' He went on to say that we know they are one of the least effective ways of conveying information, and have been made almost redundant in the age of the internet – so why give lectures? It was a tumbleweed moment. Afterwards people came up and discussed this provocation, for that was what it was, with Mike. He remembers a particular comment that given their low status, foundation year lecturers held onto giving lectures as it was one of the only things that made them feel 'proper' – a proper lecturer who gave lectures.

Students themselves can also reinscribe this view. Mike remembers showing round a group of potential foundation year students on an open day. They were a group of widening participation students with little knowledge of universities and higher education. It was when they went into a big tiered lecture hall that one of the students gasped and remarked that this was what they had been waiting for: this was a 'proper' university experience. When questioned, this perception was based on the films and shows they had seen, and the fantasies they had created, about university. Alan has had similar experiences, when occasionally youth and community students are timetabled in a lecture theatre. For staff it limits the creative way they teach, or the opportunity for more open and equal discussion without the 'teacher' having all the control and power, orchestrating and performing at the front – but the students love it: it feels like 'real' university.

Alan has a different experience; he started out teaching higher education in a large further education college. His team were successful in validating a BA (Hons) degree, the first the college had ever written itself, rather than delivered on behalf of a franchising university. He remembers working late into the night, eating pizzas with his Head of Department, as they finally completed the documentation. The next morning, he arrived late to work and there was a message from his Head of Department asking why he hadn't been in for 8:45, as was the college expectation. This experience has shaped his transition to university lecturer, and made him value (but not take for granted) the autonomy that goes with it, but perhaps it is also part of the reason he still feels less important or valued than the researchers and 'traditional academics': after all, he is only one step up from his college teaching days.

It is this combination of challenges that drives our passion to question and challenge the practices of higher education, and to try and embed some of the principles of critical pedagogy. Hopefully we have also shown that it is possible to go beyond the lecture, the pedagogue holding all the knowledge and power (and ultimately control) and enact critical pedagogy within higher education, whether in small steps or more extensively. However, it entails a cultural shift on all sides, and people being prepared to let go of their power, not easy when it is often the most powerless individuals, students and lecturers who must lead the way. Both Mike and Alan have shown that it is possible to influence change, even at a structural level, although we need to be realistic about our limitations and create the right conditions.

In many ways, critical pedagogy is a world view, an attitude, not a teaching tool. We need to keep its ideas in mind at all times and apply them in multiple ways and at multiple points. It is not enough to ask when one can use a critical pedagogy approach; one should, in any teaching and situation, or indeed any situation, ask how you can bring the principles of critical pedagogy to bear. Neoliberal thinking works by becoming all pervasive to the point where we no longer see it as an ideology, but as common sense, and just the way things are. We need therefore to establish, continually, a counter narrative that shows that things can be done differently and more easily than we sometimes think, and even more radically. We need to see critical pedagogy, or at least some acknowledgement of the inherent power imbalance, enacted and challenged throughout higher education. When a non-traditional academic is being considered for promotion, or a subject is being developed further, the scrutiny must come from enlightened individuals and those who will be involved, not those who seek to protect and perpetuate the previous elitist models.

Mike was talking to a colleague recently about the reasonable adjustments and extension regime in institutions they had worked in. They discussed how the panel or committee that considers reasonable adjustments often ends up with a group-think mentality, defending the processes and standards against the students, who are often seen as inherently deceptive and guilty unless they can prove their innocence. We then discussed how this should and could change. Mike then asked why we have deadlines at all? Who are they for? Why not let students set their own deadlines? (A practice Mike had worked to before.) Apart from an argument about students getting used to having deadlines because they would have them in life (begging more questions than it answered and only really being a justification for one assessment having an external deadline), Mike and his colleague agreed that we set deadlines mainly because we always have, and they are set largely for lecturers' convenience. (Even though Mike's experience of working under a student-determined assignment had led to a more even marking workload.)

This conversation developed further – and went on to ask why we assess students at level 4 in the way we do, given that the marks do not count, which then led to questions about grading, who does the marking and, inevitably, why we have marks at all and assess in such constrictive ways. This is critical pedagogy, and these are generative themes, which, while they may not lead to revolutionary change, they may sow the seed for this to happen.

Some concluding thoughts and steps for change

The title of this chapter is deceptive. It would be against the spirit of critical pedagogy for us to create an agenda for critical pedagogy in higher education at this point in time. This is something that must be done on a local level first. Structural change and making structural links are vital, but you cannot jump to structural change from nowhere – it has to build organically from the ground. For this reason, most of this book has focused on the first and second stages of enabling critical pedagogy. We hope you go on to the third stage, but the fourth, of building strong alliances and changing the very notion of the university, can only be done together once there are enough of us. We hope, in time, that a critical mass of critical pedagogues in higher education emerge and coalesce – and that we can seek ways to come together and create national, and indeed international, agendas for critical pedagogy and critical pedagogues.

Alan has recently delivered two sessions at his university that are informed by, or about, critical pedagogy. What emerged was that a number of individuals do indeed try and practise it in their everyday work, but they feel quite isolated and often 'hide' it from their peers. By sharing examples, and celebrating each success, the participants asked to set up a university-wide group to support each other enacting critical pedagogy in their everyday practices, located within the remit of the Centre for Learning and Teaching – from individual to local. Because Mike had delivered a short input, he was invited to join the group, a first participant from the wider academic community, beyond Leeds Beckett University, a small step towards starting a national debate and network. In the meantime, we wish to leave you with a reminder of critical pedagogy's principles, aims and approaches and some pointers, thoughts and questions, related to the steps outlined in Chapter 1. These should hopefully help you create your own agendas for the perpetual process of becoming a critical pedagogue.

Principles, aims and approaches

In Chapter 1, we set out the principles, aims and approaches of critical pedagogy in the form of a diagram (Figure 1.1). As the diagram illustrates, the principles, aims and approaches are not linear, but inform and nestle within each other. We have used them throughout the book to demonstrate how the examples we have shared relate to critical pedagogy. Keep the principles, aims and approaches in mind as you take your own steps towards critical pedagogy.

Pointer for step one: change how you teach and your relationships with students

» Explore the supposed neutrality of education with students, both in its aims and methods. Does it serve particular groups in society?

» Enable students to explore, deconstruct and reconstruct their experiences of education, and share your own journey.

» Actively acknowledge and explore the power, and illusion of power, you and the students have in the classroom.

» Put aside your supposed mastery of the subject you teach. How can you enable the students to unearth their latent and buried knowledge on the subject? Remember your role is to work on their self-belief, self-efficacy and will in doing exploration of the subject.

» Do you actively look for teachable moments in your teaching and embrace the uncharted exploration of knowledge they can lead to? How confident do you feel about being able to work in the moment rather than relying on a predetermined teaching plan?

» Always seek to link their local issues to wider social forces (generative themes) and vice-versa that explore some of the contradictions in structural forces. Remember, these contradictions are also leverage that can lead to social action.

» Can you build in social action, or the potential for it, both at a local and wider level, into your teaching?

» Simultaneously work with students to explore the tyranny of action, whereby once they are conscious of their oppression, they may feel that if they do not change everything, they have failed. Encourage them to look for acts of symbolic hope for others and to exercise humility, remembering that if change comes in their lifetime, they are lucky.

Pointers for step two: push the structure as far as you can and build alliances

» Don't see the curriculum as a straitjacket, but as a freedom. Move beyond narrowing the curriculum to what is already known, but instead seek to question and challenge the limiting factors and start to take account of our students' collective experiences. What limits your curriculum?

» Curriculum can be seen as the syllabus, or a product, but it can equally be seen as a process and a praxis (Ord, 2008).

» When looking at co-creation with students, ask yourself if it is co-creation *in* the curriculum (or classroom) or can we seek co-creation *of* the curriculum. There are examples of how this can be adopted at all sorts of levels: how might you try this?

» What are the limitations to enacting critical pedagogy within the curriculum, and who are your allies in achieving this?

» If you are a self-identifying critical pedagogue (Mahon, 2014), do not allow yourself to reject assessment wholesale. Does it not have a use to assess what learning is going on, or even issues around power? Focus on how we can make it have maximum integrity.

» Challenge yourself, and students, when they engage in gaming assessment, or learning itself. This is where we make the right noises about learning for its own sake and as an exploration, but in reality, want to maximise student marks by working the criteria for maximum effect.

» Use Keesing-Styles's (2003) characteristics of an authentic critical pedagogic approach to assessment as a checklist/points of reflection. For him assessment should:

– centre on dialogic interactions so that the roles of teacher and learner are shared, and all voices are validated;

– foster an integrated approach to theory and practice, or what Freire would preferably term as praxis – theory in action;

– value and validate the experience students bring to the classroom and importantly, situate this experience at the centre of the classroom content and process in ways that problematise it and make overt links with oppression and dominant discourses;

– reinterpret the complex ecology of relationships in the classroom to avoid oppressive power relations;

– create a negotiated curriculum, including assessment, equally owned by teachers and students.

» In particular, think about how you can involve students in developing the assessment regime, including any assessment criteria, and involve them directly in marking and moderation – there are plenty of examples of how this is possible both within a module and indeed in designing the whole programme.

» The experience of higher education, for many, is seen as transactional – with students bringing with them expectations of what they will experience, whether that is the use of lectures and seminars or the way we teach. Stella Jones-Devitt, Professor of Critical Pedagogy, recently commented that instead it should be transformational and for us that includes the way we interact with students in our teaching methodologies.

» The impact of Covid-19, and the online pivot, has forced academics to rethink how they construct their teaching, using technology-mitigated interfaces – some of these have already removed the power imbalances, but how might we maintain some of these benefits going forward?

» Effective learning requires 'scaffolding' but prior to joining higher education, many of our learners have already been indoctrinated by the inherent power imbalances that exist within teaching and learning, and also the equivalent embodiment of our 'expertise' as a power base.

Pointers for step three: be seen as a pedagogic expert, internally and externally

» Keep in mind Holloway and Sergi's (2010) ideas about crack capitalism. Find cracks and spaces in higher education, often caused by its contradictions, in which critical pedagogy can flourish, which, in time, may open up and create new opportunities and the possibility of eventual systemic change.

» Reflect on how Covid-19 has had a positive impact on student learning, in that learning can be happening in spaces that are not wholly owned by the institution and may mean that existing hierarchies can be questioned and challenged.

» Think how you can encourage students to engage with the wider consultation mechanisms of the institution, and to challenge things they do not agree with, and then to take this further with things like the Office for Students, the Student Union and other bodies that are meant to represent their interests.

» Find ways to encourage, or at least make students aware of, other campaigns they can get involved in, including ones from students' unions or more independent campaigns such as 'Why Is My Curriculum White?' 'Black Lives Matter' and 'Rhodes Must Fall'.

» If you have a critical pedagogy group, make sure its remit is not just about teaching and that it explores and engages in local issues pertinent to the whole university community. There will often be issues in common between staff (academic, professional and ancillary), students and the local community, often things like local services, transport and facilities.

» If your subject has a PSRB, does it engage students in their developmental work, and if not, can you engage students in asking them how it could? If it does, how can you encourage students to get involved in this?

» If you work in a professional subject, or even if not, how could you encourage students to get involved in the wider field and/or how could you encourage that wider field to be involved in the training and assessment of students and development of the field?

» How can you encourage students and the wider institution to engage with the community? Most university mission statements make noises about being there for the community, but what does this mean in practice and in a very local sense? Are there groups and forums that you can link in with and engage with? The institution may welcome your engagement as they are often at a loss with how to effectively engage and are looking for leadership.

» Engage in debates at your institution about what is the purpose of the university. This is often done when a new strategic plan is being developed. Also engage in how these consultations processes are being enacted. Is there scope to influence them?

» Similarly participate in the development of the institution's mission statement and aims, etc. While often just statements, they can become leverage, particularly if you are trying to bring in a new initiative – these are the institution's espoused values, so refer back to them.

» Try and act within a collective, both because it means you are influencing others and can avoid being picked off as an individual. You can often set up such groups under the institution's Centre for Learning and Teaching, or equivalent. If this is not possible, just set one up anyway. Could the institution really stop you doing this?

» Do not be seduced by becoming the token radical or maverick. These roles are useful to institutions to show the diversity of opinions they have, but they are rarely influential.

» Remember spaces for critical pedagogy are not always easy. Beware of the safe space, or more accurately look at how safety is being defined and by whom. Pedagogical spaces are often emotional, visceral and edgy, although if outright dangerous they may not be productive.

» Use both Mahon's (2014) list of enablers and disablers in institutions, and her list of institutional conditions for critical pedagogy to thrive in universities, as checklists and things to lobby the institution with, to enable critical pedagogy to meaningfully develop.

Final word

As ever, the real dynamic seems to lie at the intersection of structure and agency. In order to enact critical pedagogy, we need to reflect on our motivations and intents and build practice architectures that enable critical pedagogy collectively. There is a need to have a community of practice, and not act in isolation. When the seemingly all-pervasive market and neoliberal approaches to higher education collapse under the weight of their own irrationality, critical pedagogues need to be waiting in the wings with new answers and vision.

References

Aliakbari, M and Faraji, E (2011) Basic Principles of Critical Pedagogy. Paper presented at 2nd *International Conference on Humanities, Historical and Social Sciences* IPEDR vol 17.

Alinsky, S D (1989) *Rules for Radicals: A Practical Primer for Realistic Radicals*. London: Vintage.

Altbach, P G, Reisberg, L and Rumbley, L E (2009) Trends in Global Higher Education: Tracking an Academic Revolution (A Report Prepared for the UNESCO 2009 World Conference on Higher Education). [online] Available at: http://atepie.cep.edu.rs/public/Altbach,_Reisberg,_Rumbley_Tracking_an_Academic_Revolution,_UNESCO_2009.pdf (accessed 25 June 2021).

Aristotle (1976) *The Nicomachean Ethics*. Harmondsworth: Penguin.

Augar, P (2019) *Independent Panel Report: Post-18 Review of Education and Funding*. HMSO: London.

Baizerman, M (1989) Why Train Youth Workers? *The Child Care Worker*, 7(1): 1–8.

Ball, S J (2012) Performativity, Commodification and Commitment: An I-spy Guide to the Neoliberal University. *British Journal of Educational Studies*, 60(1): 17–28.

Bardy, H and Gilsenan, M (2021) Preparing for an Unexpected Journey: Exploring the Experience of Teaching Critical Pedagogy through Critical Pedagogy. In Seal, M (ed) (2021) *Hopeful Pedagogies in Higher Education*. London: Bloomsbury.

Barros, S R (2011) Terms of Engagement: Reframing Freirean-based Assessment in Institutional Education. *Rangsit Journal of Arts and Sciences*, 1: 79–87.

Batsleer, J (2012) *What Is Youth Work?* London: Learning Matters.

Benjamin, J (2017) *Beyond Doer and Done to: Recognition Theory, Intersubjectivity and the Third*. London: Routledge.

Bleiklie, I (1998) Justifying the Evaluative State: New Pubic Management Ideals in Higher Education. *European Journal of Education*, 33(2): 299–316.

Bolton, G (2010) *Reflective Practice, Writing and Professional Development* (3rd ed). Thousand Oaks, CA: SAGE Publications.

Bovill, C (2014) An Investigation of Co-created Curricula within Higher Education in the UK, Ireland and the USA. *Innovations in Education and Teaching International*, 51(1): 15–25.

Bovill, C (2020) Co-creating Learning and Teaching: Towards Relational Pedagogy in Higher Education. St Albans: Critical Publishing.

Bovill, C and Woolmer, C (2019) How Conceptualisations of Curriculum in Higher Education Influence Student Staff Co-Creation in and of the Curriculum. *Higher Education*, 78(3): 407–22.

Braa, D and Callero, P (2006) Critical Pedagogy and Classroom Praxis. *Teaching Sociology*, 34(4): 357–69.

Breunig, M (2005) Turning Experiential Education and Critical Pedagogy Theory into Praxis. *The Journal of Experiential Education*, 28(2): 106–23.

Brito, I, Lima, A and Auerbach, E (2004) The Logic of Nonstandard Teaching: A Course in Cape Verdean Language, Culture, and History. In Norton, B and Toohey, K (eds) *Critical Pedagogies and Language Learning* (pp 181–200). Cambridge: Cambridge University Press.

Bullen, E, Kenway, J and Fahey, J (2010) The Knowledge Economy and Research Governance: How We Got to Where We Are. In Blackmore, J, Brennan, M and Zipin, L (eds) *Re-positioning University Governance and Academic Work* (pp 53–66). Rotterdam: Sense.

Burbules, N C and Berk, R (1999) Critical Thinking and Critical Pedagogy: Relations, Differences, and Limits. In Popkewitz, T S (ed) *Critical Theories in Education: Changing Terrains of Knowledge and Politics* (pp 45–65). New York: Routledge.

Butler, J (1990) *Gender Trouble*. New York: Routledge.

Canham, N (2017) Comparing Web 2.0 Applications for Peer Feedback in Language Teaching: Google Docs, the Sakai VLE, and the Sakai Wiki. *Writing & Pedagogy*, 9(3): 429–56.

Canham, N, Dixon, K, Golby, B, Gorman, S, Imeson, S, Muskett, T and Scranage, J (2017) Popular Education in Practice: A Case Study of Radical Educational Praxis in a Contemporary UK University. In Seal, M (ed) *Trade Union Education: Transforming the World* (pp 216–27). Oxford: New Internationalist.

Carr, W and Kemmis, S (1989) *Becoming Critical: Education, Knowledge and Action Research*. Lewes: Falmer.

Chambers, R (2002) *Relaxed and Participatory Appraisal: Notes on Practical Approaches and Methods for Participants in PRA/PLA-Related Familiarisation Workshops*. Participation Group, Institute of Development Studies, University of Sussex.

Chambers, R (2010) A Revolution Whose Time Has Come? The Win–Win of Quantitative Participatory Approaches and Methods. *IDS Bulletin*, 41(6), 45–55.

Cornwall, A (2003) Whose Voices? Whose Choices? Reflections on Gender and Participatory Development. *World Development* 31(8): 1325–42.

Cho, S (2010) Politics of Critical Pedagogy and New Social Movements. *Educational Philosophy and Theory*, 42(3): 310–25.

Clark, L B (2018) Critical Pedagogy in the University: Can a Lecture Be Critical Pedagogy? *Policy Futures in Education*, 16(8): 985–99.

Cooke, B and Kothari, U (eds) (2001) *Participation: The New Tyranny?* London: Zed Books.

Cooper, C (2015) Critical Pedagogy in Higher Education. In Cooper, C, Gormally, S and Hughes, G (eds) *Socially Just, Radical Alternatives for Education and Youth Work Practice* (pp 39–64). London: Palgrave Macmillan.

Costandius E and Blitzer E (eds) (2015) *Engaging Higher Education Curricula*. Stellenbosch: Sun Press.

Cowden, S and Singh, G (2013) *Acts of Knowing: Critical Pedagogy in, Against and Beyond the University*. London: Bloomsbury Publishing.

Davies, B and Bansel, P (2005) The Time of Their Lives? Academic Workers in Neoliberal Time(s). *Health Sociology Review*, 14(1): 47–58.

Davies, B and Bansel, P (2007) Neoliberalism and Education. *International Journal of Qualitative Studies in Education*, 20(3): 247–59.

Davies, R (2012) *Youth Work, 'Protest' and a Common Language: Towards a Framework for Reasoned Debate*, paper delivered at the annual conference of the Professional Association of Lecturers in Youth and Community Work 2012, Lake District.

DCLG (2010) Communities and Local Government Committee on the Government's Plans for Localism and Decentralisation. [online] Available at: https://publications.parliament.uk/pa/cm201011/cmselect/cmcomloc/writev/localism/localism.pdf (accessed 25 June 2021).

Degener, S (2001) Making Sense of Critical Pedagogy in Adult Literacy Education. *Review of Adult Learning and Literacy*, 2(2): 23–45.

Edwards, C (1983) Student-Centred Learning and Trade Union Education: A Preliminary Examination. *The Industrial Tutor*, 3(8): 45–54.

Engstrom, C L (2008) Autoethnography as an Approach to Intercultural Training. *Rocky Mountain Communication Review*, 4(2): 17–31.

Eraut, M (2004) Informal Learning in the Workplace. *Studies in Continuing Education*, 26(2): 247–73.

Fals-Borda, O and Rahman, M A (1991) *Action and Knowledge: Breaking the Monopoly with Participatory Action-Research*. New York: Apex Press.

Fiorenza, E (2009) Introduction: Exploring the Intersections of Race, Gender, Status and Ethnicity in Early Christian Studies. In Nasrallah, L and Schüssler Fiorenza, E (eds) *Prejudice and Christian Beginnings: Investigating Race, Gender, and Ethnicity in Early Christian Studies* (pp 1–25). Minneapolis, MN: Fortress Press.

Foley, P (2007) A Case for and of Critical Pedagogy: Meeting the Challenge of Liberatory Education at Gallaudet University. Paper presented at the *American Communication Association's* annual conference. Taos, NM.

Freire, P (1968) *Pedagogy of the Oppressed* (translated by Ramos, M B). New York: Herder and Herder.

Freire, P (1970a) *Cultural Action for Freedom*. London: Penguin.

Freire, P (1970b) Cultural Action and Conscientization. *Harvard Educational Review*, 40(3): 452–77.

Freire, P (1974) *Education: The Practice of Freedom*. London: Writers and Readers Publishing Cooperative.

Freire, P (1990) Educational Practice. In Horton, M and Freire, P (eds) *We Make the Road by Walking: Conversations on Education and Social Change* (pp 145–97). Philadelphia, PA: Temple University Press.

Freire, P (1996) *Letters to Cristina: Reflections on My Life and Work* (translated by Macedo, D, Macedo, Q and Oliveira, A). New York: Routledge.

Freire, P (2004) *Pedagogy of Hope: Reliving Pedagogy of the Oppressed*. London: Bloomsbury Publishing.

Ghaye, T, Melander-Wikman, A, Kisare, M, Chambers, P, Bergmark, U, Kostenius, C and Lillyman, S (2008) Participatory and Appreciative Action and Reflection (PAAR): Democratizing Reflective Practices. *Reflective Practice*, 9(4), 361–97.

Gibbs, P, Angelides, P and Michaelides, P (2004) Preliminary Thoughts on a Praxis of Higher Education Teaching. *Teaching in Higher Education*, 9(2): 183–94.

Gillespie, D, Ashbaugh, L and DeFiore, J (2002) White Woman Teaching White Women about White Privilege, Race Cognizance and Social Action: Toward a Pedagogical Pragmatics. *Race Ethnicity and Education*, 5(3): 237–53.

Giroux, H A (2005) The Terror of Neoliberalism: Rethinking the Significance of Cultural Politics. *College Literature*, 32(1): 1–19.

Giroux, H A (2010) Bare Pedagogy and the Scourge of Neoliberalism: Rethinking Higher Education as a Democratic Public Sphere. *Educational Forum*, 74(3): 184–96.

Giroux, H A (2012) Higher Education under Siege: Rethinking the Politics of Critical Pedagogy. *Counterpoints* 422: 327–41.

Giroux, H A (2017) Neoliberalism's War against Higher Education and the Role of Public Intellectuals. In Izak, M, Kostera, M and Zawadzki, M (eds) *The Future of University Education* (pp 185–206). Cham: Springer.

Giroux, H A (2018) *Terror of Neoliberalism: Authoritarianism and the Eclipse of Democracy*. New York: Routledge.

Giroux, H A and Giroux, S S (2006) Challenging Neoliberalism's New World Order: The Promise of Critical Pedagogy. *Cultural Studies, Critical Methodologies*, 6(1): 21–32.

Green, B (2012) Addressing the Curriculum Problem in Doctoral Education. *Australian Universities' Review*, 54(1): 10–18.

Habermas, J (1989) *The New Conservatism: Cultural Criticism and the Historians' Debate*. Cambridge, MA: MIT Press.

Hardy, I (2010) Teacher Talk: Flexible Delivery and Academics' Praxis in an Australian University. *International Journal for Academic Development*, 15(2): 131–42.

Harris, P (2014) The Youth Worker as Jazz Improviser: Foregrounding Education 'in the Moment' within the Professional Development of Youth Workers. *Professional Development in Education*, 40(4): 654–68.

Harris, P, Haywood, C and Mac an Ghaill, M (2017) Higher Education, De-centred Subjectivities and the Emergence of a Pedagogical Self Among Black and Muslim Students. *Race Ethnicity and Education*, 20(3): 358–71.

Hartman, Y and Darab, S (2012) A Call for Slow Scholarship: A Case Study on the Intensification of Academic Life and Its Implications for Pedagogy. *Review of Education, Pedagogy, and Cultural Studies*, 34(1–2): 49–60.

Hartmann, T (2000) *Complete Guide to ADHD*. Grass Valley: Underwood Books.

Heron, J (1996) *Co-operative Inquiry: Research into the Human Condition*. London: Sage.

Hills, M, Mullett, J and Carroll, S (2000) Community-based Research: Creating Evidence-based Practice for Health and Social Care. *Pan American Journal of Public Heath* 21: 125–35.

Holloway, J and Sergi, V (2010) *Crack Capitalism* (Vol 40). London: Pluto Press.

hooks, b (1994) *Teaching to Transgress: Education as the Practice of Freedom*. New York: Routledge Falmer.

Jacobs, H L M (2008) Perspectives on Information Literacy and Reflective Pedagogical Praxis. *The Journal of Academic Librarianship*, 34(3): 256–62.

Jeffs, T and Smith, M K (1999) *Informal Education: Conversation, Democracy and Learning*, 3rd ed. Nottingham: Educational Heretics Press.

Jeyaraj, J J (2020) Possibilities for Critical Pedagogy Engagement in Higher Education: Exploring Students' Openness and Acceptance. *Asia Pacific Education Review*, 21(1): 27–38.

Joldersma, C (1999) The Tension between Justice and Freedom in Paulo Freire's Epistemology. *Journal of Educational Thought*, 35(2): 129–48.

Kahl Jr, D H (2013) Critical Communication Pedagogy and Assessment: Reconciling Two Seemingly Incongruous Ideas. *International Journal of Communication*, 7: 21–32.

Keesing-Styles, L (2003) The Relationship between Critical Pedagogy and Assessment in Teacher Education. *Radical Pedagogy*, 5(1): 1–19.

Kemmis, S and Grootenboer, P (2008) Situating Praxis in Practice: Practice Architectures and the Cultural, Social and Material Conditions for Practice. In Kemmis, S and Smith, T (eds) *Enabling Praxis: Challenges for Education* (pp 37–62). Rotterdam: Sense.

Kesby, M, Kindon, S and Pain, R (2007) *Participatory Action Research Approaches and Methods*. London: Routledge.

Kincheloe, J (2005) *Critical Pedagogy*. New York: Peter Lang.

KPMG (2020) *The Future of Higher Education in a Disruptive World*. London: KPMG.

Kumashiro, K (2002) *Troubling Education: Queer Activism and Anti-Oppressive Pedagogy*. New York: Routledge Falmer.

Lee, A and Dunston, R (2011) Practice, Learning and Change: Towards a Re-theorisation of Professional Education. *Teaching in Higher Education*, 16(5): 483–94.

Mahon, K (2014) *Critical Pedagogical Praxis in Higher Education*. Unpublished PhD thesis, Charles Stuart University.

Markus, H and Nurius, P (1986) Possible Selves. *American Psychologist*, 41(9): 954–69.

McLaren, P (1999) Research News and Comment: A Pedagogy of Possibility: Reflecting upon Paulo Freire's Politics of Education: In Memory of Paulo Freire. *Educational Researcher*, 28(2): 49–56.

McLoughlin, T, Randolf, L and Seal, M (2021) University as Community: Breaking the Circle of Certainty. In Seal, M (ed) *Hopeful Pedagogies in Higher Education*. London: Bloomsbury.

Mignolo, W D (2009) Epistemic Disobedience, Independent Thought and Decolonial Freedom. *Theory, Culture & Society*, 26(7–8): 159–81.

MillionPlus (2016) *Policy Briefing: Is Science and Research Funding in Higher Education Meeting the Challenges of the 21st Century?* London: MillionPlus.

Motta, S (2013) Pedagogies of Possibility In, Against and Beyond the Imperial Patriarchal Subjectivities of Higher Education. In Cowden, S and Singh, G (eds) *Acts of Knowing: Critical Pedagogy In, Against and Beyond the University* (pp 82–124). London: Bloomsbury.

Muskett T A (2017) Popular Education in Practice: A Case Study of Radical Educational Praxis in a Contemporary UK University. In Seal, M (ed) *Trade Union Education: Transforming the World* (pp 216–27). Oxford: New Internationalist.

Neary, M and Winn, J (2009) The Student as Producer: Reinventing the Student Experience in Higher Education. In Bell, L, Neary, M and Stevenson, H (eds) *The Future of Higher Education: Policy, Pedagogy and the Student Experience* (pp 192–210). London: Bloomsbury Publishing.

Neelands, J (2011) Drama as Creative Learning. In Sefton-Green, J, Thomson, P, Jones, K and Bresler, L (eds) *The Routledge International Handbook of Creative Learning* (pp 168–77). London: Routledge.

Nicholls, D (2017) Reviving Trade Union and Popular Education. [online] Available at: https://indefenceofyouthwork.com/2017/02/23/doug-nicholls-on-reviving-trade-union-and-popular-education (accessed 10 April 2021).

Nixon, J (2011) *Higher Education and the Public Good: Imagining the University.* London: Continuum.

Ohara, M, Saft, S and Crookes, G (2000) Teacher Exploration of Feminist Critical Pedagogy in Beginning Japanese as a Foreign Language Class. Paper presented at the University of Hawaii, Manoa.

Ord, J (2000) *Youth Work Curriculum.* Lyme Regis: Russell House.

Ord, J (2008) A Curriculum for Youth Work: The Experience of the English Youth Service. *Youth Studies Australia,* 27(4): 16–24.

Owen, H (2008) *Open Space Technology: A User's Guide.* San Francisco, CA: Berrett-Koehler Publishers.

Parkes, S, Mathias, L and Seal, M (2018) Becoming a Newman Foundation Year Student: Conscientization to Promote Democratic Engagement, Meaningful Dialogue and Co-operative Working. *Journal of the Foundation Year Network,* 1: 71–86.

Pegg, A and Carr, J (2010) Articulating Learning and Supporting Student Employability: Using the Concept of 'Illusio' to Make Sense of the Issues Raised by Distance Learners. *Widening Participation and Lifelong Learning,* 12(2): 78–90.

Quinn, J (2010) *Learning Communities and Imagined Social Capital.* London: Continuum Studies in Educational Research.

Rancière, J (1991) *The Ignorant Schoolmaster* (Vol 1). Stanford, CA: Stanford University Press.

Rancière, J (1992) *The Ignorant Schoolmaster: Five Lessons in Intellectual Emancipation.* Stanford, CA: Stanford University Press.

Savan, B and Sider, D (2003) Contrasting Approaches to Community-based Research and a Case Study of Community Sustainability in Toronto, Canada. *Local Environment,* 8(3): 303–16.

Schugurensky, D (2014) *Paulo Freire.* London: Bloomsbury Publishing.

Seal, M (2014) Philosophies of Youth Work: Post-Modern Chameleons or Cherry-Picking Charlatans. In Seal, M and Frost, S (eds) *Philosophy and Youth and Community Work* (pp 145–56). Lyme Regis: Russell House.

Seal, M (2018) *Participatory Pedagogic Impact Research: Community Involvement in Action.* London: Routledge.

Seal, M (2019) *Interrupting Heteronormativity in Higher Education: Critical Queer Pedagogies.* London: Palgrave Macmillan.

Seal, M (ed) (2021) *Hopeful Pedagogies in Higher Education: Dancing in the Cracks.* Londom: Bloomsbury Press.

Seal, M and Frost, S (2014) *Philosophy and Youth and Community Work.* Lyme Regis: Russell House.

Seal, M and Harris, P (2014) I Just Talk to People. In Seal, M and Frost, S (eds) *Philosophy and Youth and Community Work* (pp 90–112). Lyme Regis: Russell House.

Seal, M and Parkes, S (2019) Pedagogy as Transition: Student Directed Tutor Groups on Foundation Years. *Journal of the Foundation Year Network*, 2: 7–20.

Schön, D (1987) *Educating the Reflective Practitioner.* San Francisco, CA: Jossey-Bass.

Serrano, M M, O'Brien, M, Roberts, K and Whyte, D (2018) Critical Pedagogy and Assessment in Higher Education: The Ideal of 'Authenticity' in Learning. *Active Learning in Higher Education*, 19(1): 9–21.

Servaes, J, Jacobson, T L and White, S A (eds) (1996) Participatory Communication for Social Change. London: Sage.

Shor, I (1992) *Empowering Education: Critical Teaching for Social Change.* Chicago, IL: University of Chicago Press.

Shor, I and Freire, P (1987) *A Pedagogy for Liberation: Dialogues on Transforming Education.* New York: Greenwood Publishing Group.

Shore, C and Wright, S (2004) Whose Accountability? Governmentality and the Auditing of Universities. *Parallax*, 10(2): 100–16.

Smith, F (1995) Let's Declare Education a Disaster and Get on with Our Lives. *Phi Delta Kappan*, 76: 584–90.

Smith, L T (1999) *Decolonizing Methodologies: Research and Indigenous Peoples.* London: Zed Books.

Smith, M K (1994) *Local Education.* Buckingham: Open University Press.

Taylor, P (1993) *The Texts of Paulo Freire.* Buckingham: Open University Press.

Trelfa, J (2016) Whatever Happened to 'Reflective Practice'? In Current Issues and New Thoughts on Reflective Practice. *Journal of Research Institute*, 53: 79–102.

Van Heertum, R (2006) Marcuse, Bloch and Freire: Reinvigorating a Pedagogy of Hope. *Policy Futures in Education*, 4(1): 45–51.

Walker, M (2002) Pedagogy and the Politics and Purposes of Higher Education. *Arts and Humanities in Higher Education*, 1(1): 43–58.

Webb, D (2010) Paulo Freire and the Need for a Kind of Education in Hope. *Cambridge Journal of Education*, 40(4): 327–39.

Index